Praise for *The I*

"Nobody reports on the treasures and traumas of public education better than John Merrow. He is, quite simply, the leading education journalist in America. Anybody who doubts that should read this book. John gets it. And he tells it straight, cleanly and evenly – with color and grace."
– Jim Lehrer, Anchor, PBS NewsHour

"In The *Influence of Teachers,* John Merrow draws on years of his own research, observations, and conversations about education to share what he's learned. As always, his thoughtful insights are invaluable for anyone concerned about children and the future of American education."
– Marian Wright Edelman, President, Children's Defense Fund

"No one knows our schools and understands the fierce debates over them better than John Merrow, and no one parses those controversies with more humaneness and perceptiveness. 'If you can keep your head when all about you are losing theirs' could be the motto of this fine book. If only there were more John Merrows!" *– E. D. Hirsch, Jr., Founder, Core Knowledge, and author of Cultural Literacy*

"*The Influence of Teachers* is a warm and thoughtful tribute to teachers, as well as a call to action from the dean of American education reporters. This short volume packs punch, with lots of stories from John Merrow's 35 years of reporting. *The Influence of Teachers* is both important and enjoyable."
– Richard C. Riley, U.S. Secretary of Education (1992-2000)

"From our experience as educators, we know the remarkable change that can happen when great teachers and innovative leaders combine forces. In *The Influence of Teachers,* John Merrow explores the complex, ever-changing relationship between the teachers in our classrooms and the officials who lead them. What

he describes is fundamental to changing the face of public education in this country."
– *Mike Feinberg and Dave Levin, Co-founders of KIPP (Knowledge Is Power Program)*

"This book reveals the grand arc of John Merrow's career--still unfinished--and of his profound interest in and affection for schooling and schools, and for the students and teachers who inhabit them."
– *Larry Rosenstock, Founder of High Tech High & 2010 McGraw Prize in Education recipient*

"*The Influence of Teachers* rejects the finger pointing and noise-making of the policymakers and calls for a focus on the real challenge – the need for education to catch up with the changes in student needs that science and technology have wrought. Concise, clear, rare, and most important!"
– *Dr. James Comer, MD, Maurice Falk Professor of Child Psychiatry, Yale School of Medicine*

"With passion and wisdom, John Merrow lays out what is required – great teachers and leaders – to solve the most pressing need in America, to educate our children. We have no excuse but to meet this challenge and now have Merrow's further inspiration and insight to guide us, based upon a life of reporting and teaching. This is a book that will move you to tears and to action."
– *Anthony Marx, President, Amherst College and incoming President, New York Public Library*

"Once again, John Merrow has given us a rich collection of portraits from the schools blended with his lively commentary. Whether you nod in agreement or argue with it, you will keep turning the pages of this provocative book."
– *Mike Rose, Author of Why School? and Lives on the Boundary*

"John Merrow's wonderfully wise and highly readable book offers fresh insights that challenge the ideologies of education reformers everywhere. With a laser-like focus on what makes for good

teaching, it is 'must' reading for policymakers and practitioners alike."
—Tony Wagner, Innovation Education Fellow, Technology & Entrepreneurship Center at Harvard, and author of The Global Achievement Gap

"In this passionate, persuasive and eminently readable book, John Merrow argues that, to transform our public education system, we must create learning environments where teachers can be truly nurturing, collaborative, and accountable; and where all our children – no matter what their socio-economic background – feel emotionally safe and intellectually stimulated. Anyone seriously interested in school reform should read this book."
– Christopher Cerf, co-creator, Between the Lions (PBS), & 2010 McGraw Prize in Education recipient

"John Merrow has spent decades looking deeply inside American educational reform movements, fads, failures, and effective classrooms and schools. He makes his observations and insights accessible in a truly interesting and thought-provoking book that raises all the important questions and also points to some answers. He takes the reader through the stories of various educational leaders carrying out one interesting experiment after another. I learned a lot and enjoyed the read."
– Dorothy Stoneman, Founder of Youthbuild

"A stunningly balanced and penetrating analysis of our schools and the challenges we face in fixing them by one of the greatest commentators on education our country has. Let's move beyond simplistic slams about who is to blame and understand the complex set of constraints we face in transforming our schools and honoring and unleashing our teachers. John Merrow takes us on a most important journey toward that end. And it is a great read."
– John Seely Brown, author of A New Culture of Learning & former Director of Xerox Palo Alto Research Center (PARC)

"John Merrow's incisive observations and powerful, moving stories in his new book, *The Influence of Teachers: Reflections on*

Teaching and Leadership, are prescient at a time when the public is searching for solutions to America's systemic educational challenges. His dedication 'To Outstanding Teachers Everywhere,' and his preface 'Fighting the Last War' foreshadow the problems and solutions that the book richly develops. A 'must read' for those responsible for American's children and their future: that would be all of us."
– *Patrick Bassett, Executive Director, The National Association of Independent Schools*

"In 1948, Adlai Stevenson could say with justice, 'The most American thing about America is the free common school system.' Not today, with public education distressingly uneven, defined by the geography of wealth and race, feeding a nation of the rising rich and the sinking middle class. No one has tracked this decline and the struggle to reverse it with more zeal or a clearer mind than John Merrow. His biting conclusions make this book bitter but instructive reading."
– *Robert MacNeil, author of Wordstruck & former anchor, The MacNeil/Lehrer NewsHour*

"In *The Influence of Teachers*, John Merrow writes with passion and conviction about teachers, a group uniquely positioned to have a "lasting impression" on the lives of learners. Drawing on his vast interactions with students and educators – as well as on his own experiences as a teacher – Merrow's central message is that we need to shift our focus, from adults to children, to make progress as a nation. His timely recommendations on how to make teaching a 'better job' for 'better people' go to the heart of the problem."
–*Kathleen McCartney, Dean & Gerald S. Lesser Professor in Early Childhood Development, Harvard Graduate School of Education*

"Although I don't agree with all of John Merrow's conclusions, he does capture the public education debate quite well. While all sides understand the importance of teachers, Merrow points out the need to support, not bash, teachers if we want to realize the hope we place in them to educate our nation's children as well rounded, creative citizens. He also asks the teachers unions to focus more on how to support, and less on how to protect, their members. We are up to that challenge, but we can't do it alone. Education leaders in this country must walk that walk as well, taking mutual responsibility rather than simply focusing on test scores and individual teacher accountability."

— *Randi Weingarten, President, American Federation of Teachers*

ALSO BY JOHN MERROW

Choosing Excellence: "Good Enough" Schools Are Not Good Enough (2001)

Declining by Degrees: Higher Education at Risk (edited with Richard Hersh, 2005)

Below C Level: How American Education Encourages Mediocrity, and What We Can Do about It (2010)

The Influence of Teachers: Reflections on Teaching and Leadership

John Merrow

LM Books
A division of Learning Matters, Inc.
New York, N.Y.

LM Books
A division of Learning Matters, Inc.

Published in the United States of America by LM Books.
127 West 26th Street #1200, New York, N.Y. 10001
www.learningmatters.tv

© 2011 John Merrow

ISBN-13: 978-0615431727
ISBN-10: 0615431720

Dedicated to outstanding
teachers everywhere

CONTENTS

Acknowledgments

Esther Wojcicki, the brilliant journalism teacher at Palo Alto High School (and a member of the Learning Matters Board), insisted that I write this book.

Anique Halliday, Amanda Morales and Carmen Rojas, my colleagues at Learning Matters, guided the editorial process with intelligence, insight, persistence and humor.

As he has so often done with my efforts at writing, my good friend Ray Bacchetti provided a thoughtful analysis of the manuscript, including many general and specific suggestions, most of which I have tried to follow.

Much of the credit for this book's virtues belongs to these five individuals. The flaws and omissions that remain are my responsibility.

Preface

Fighting the Last War

"Microfiche," the 14-year-old asked, staring at the machines tucked away in the New York Public Library? "What's microfiche?"

How many people under age 30 could explain it? Her question is a powerful reminder of how technology has turned learning on its head. Just a few years ago, libraries and schools were the places that stored knowledge - on microfiche, in the Encyclopedia Britannica, and in the heads of the adults in charge. We had to go there to gain access to that knowledge.

Not any more. Today knowledge and information are everywhere, 24/7, thanks to the Internet. Unless libraries have been closed because of budget cuts, they have adapted to this new world. Most have become multi-purpose centers with Internet access that distribute books, audio books and DVD's. Librarians encourage patrons to ask questions, because they need to keep the public coming through their doors.

By contrast, schools remain a monopoly, places where children are expected to answer questions, by filling in the bubbles or blanks and by speaking up when called upon.

Providing access to knowledge, one of three historical justifications for schools, no longer applies in the usual sense. Of course, children need teachers to help them learn to read and master numbers, but, beyond that, a new approach is required. More about that later.

A second justification, socialization, has also been turned on its head by technology. Today's kids don't need school for socialization in the usual sense of learning to get along with their peers in the building. Why? Because there are online places for that, dozens of them, including Facebook, FarmVille, My Space and so on, and so 'socialization' takes on new meanings when kids routinely text with 'friends they've never met' across the continent or an ocean. Again, schools must adapt to this new reality.

Only custodial care, the third historical justification for school, remains unchanged. Parents still need places to send their children to keep them safe. So does the larger society, which has rejected child labor and does not want kids on the streets.

But when schools provide *only* custodial care and a marginal education that denies technology's reach and power, young people walk away, as at least 6,000 do every school day, for an annual dropout total of over 1 million.

And some of those who *remain* in marginal schools will find themselves in danger, because the youthful energy that ought to be devoted to meaningful learning will inevitably be released, somewhere. Often it comes out in bullying, cyberbullying and other forms of child abuse by children. That is, marginal education often produces dangerous schools.

Unfortunately, those in charge of public education have not been paying attention to these seismic changes. Instead they are warring over teacher competence, test scores, merit pay and union rules, issues that are fundamentally irrelevant to the world children live in.

Who are these warriors?

On one side in this battle is a cadre of prominent superintendents and wealthy hedge fund managers. Led by New York Schools Chancellor Joel Klein and D.C. Chancellor Michelle Rhee, 15 leading school superintendents issued a 1379-word manifesto in October 2010 asserting that the difficulty of removing incompetent teachers "has left our school districts impotent and, worse, has robbed millions of children of a real future."

This side believes in charter schools, Teach for America, and paying teachers based on their students' test scores. Publicly pushing this "free market" line is a powerful trio: Davis Guggenheim's *Waiting for Superman* movie; NBC's semi-journalistic exercise, Education Nation; and Oprah Winfrey. And if one movie isn't enough, this side also has *The Lottery* in the wings.

It has identified the villains: bad teachers and the evil unions that protect them, particularly Randi Weingarten of the American Federation of Teachers.

The other side is clearly outnumbered: The National Education Association and the American Federation of Teachers, the two teacher unions; many teachers and some Democrats. Its villains are No Child Left Behind and its narrow focus on bubble test scores in reading and math. This side's far weaker megaphone is wielded by historian Diane Ravitch, a former Bush education policymaker turned apostate. Ravitch has been particularly critical of Bill Gates and Eli Broad, whom she refers to as 'the billionaire boys club.'

Ironically, the two billionaires are supporting *both* sides. Each, through his foundation, put money behind Guggenheim's movie and Education Nation, NBC's 3-day meeting in October 2010 that essentially echoed the free market line about charter schools and bad unions. However, the Gates Foundation is also spending millions to promote union/school board collaboration in Hillsborough, Florida, and elsewhere. As for Broad, it spends millions training school leaders; what's more, the 2010 prestigious Broad Prize in Urban Education went to a school district that is being sued by its state for *refusing* to allow charter schools.

Education Secretary Arne Duncan publicly supports both sides. He endorsed *Waiting for Superman* and played a prominent role in Education Nation, but he also presented the Broad Prize and defends Randi Weingarten.

Both sides ignore reality. The free market crowd's enthusiasm for charter schools sidesteps data showing that only 17 percent of the country's 4,900 charter schools outperform their public counterparts, while 37 percent significantly under perform

7

comparable public schools. On the other side, the powerful NEA continues to insist that teachers be paid based on years of service, despite overwhelming evidence that those days are over, now that everyone else from President Obama on down insists that student learning matters more than a teacher's experience.

But what's most striking about this bitter battle is its irrelevance. The adults in charge are fighting the last war, and whoever wins doesn't really matter to the millions of young people now being denied on a daily basis the learning opportunities that modern technology affords.

Our young people should be learning how to deal with the flood of information that surrounds them. They need guidance separating wheat from chaff. They need help formulating questions, and they need to develop the habit of seeking answers, not regurgitating them. They should be going to schools where they are expected and encouraged to discover, build, and cooperate.

Instead, most of them endure what I call 'regurgitation education' and are stuck in institutions that expect them to memorize the periodic table, the names of 50 state capitals and the major rivers of the United States.

Introduction

I began as a teacher, at a public high school in Port Washington, New York, just outside New York City. I ended up there only because I had failed the physical for the Peace Corps and could not fulfill my assignment, teaching English in Kenya. I stayed at Schreiber High School for two school years, 64-65, and 65-66.

After a short break to get my Master's Degree, I taught for two more years, this time at Virginia State College, a historically black institution in Petersburg, VA. In the evenings I taught English at the federal penitentiary in the adjoining town.

I was a TA at Harvard while in graduate school there, and for two summers I taught junior high school.

Teaching at all these levels was in many ways the most energizing work I have ever done, and I remain in awe of the men and women who dedicate their professional lives to this important work.

Shortly after I went to work for the *MacNeil/Lehrer NewsHour* in 1985, Robin MacNeil took me to lunch. While I don't remember where we ate, I've never forgotten a piece of advice Robin offered. Good ideas are rare, he said. Whenever you have one, use it in as many ways as you can. Produce a piece for us, write an op-ed or an article, and put it in a book.

The book you are holding indicates that I took Robin's good counsel to heart. Most of its chapters began as stories for the *NewsHour* or as opinion pieces for a newspaper. A few chapters grew out of events in my life, most notably a reunion of students I taught in high school in the late 1960s. A few others started as *NewsHour* stories, became op-ed pieces, morphed into posts for my weekly blog, *Taking Note,* and subsequently were deepened and improved by readers' comments. Welcome to the brave new world of interactive book writing!

I wish I'd received Robin's advice earlier (or had figured it out on my own) because I might have written something worthwhile about the reporting I was doing along the way. In 1977 I became the first National Public Radio reporter to get into China when I snuck in as a tourist with a group of Canadians, but I never wrote about it. In 1981 I spent three months in juvenile prisons but didn't write about it. In 1980 I spent several months in mental hospitals for children and juveniles but didn't think to write about it. I bonded with book burners in West Virginia in 1975 and reported on the plight of gay kids and gay teachers in 1976, but, again, wrote nothing. I probably should have written about getting the two presidents of the warring teachers unions into the same studio for a radio debate in the mid-1970s, but I didn't do that either.

iii

I have been reporting about education for NPR and PBS since 1974. I've visited every state and a dozen countries. I've gone beyond the boundaries of the schoolyard to report on prenatal care, re-education for jobless adults, the "learning" that occurs in prisons, and other issues involving young people. Along the way I have spent countless hours watching teachers at work or following educational leaders like Michelle Rhee in Washington, D.C., Joel Klein in New York City, David Hornbeck in Philadelphia, Randi Weingarten, Diana Porter in Cincinnati and Paul Vallas in Chicago, Philadelphia and New Orleans.

I admire those who have chosen to dedicate their working lives to public education, working in systems that regularly fail to acknowledge their hard work and too often beat them down with a steady diet of small humiliations.

iv

Over the years I have noticed that the best schools and the best teachers ask of every child, "How are you intelligent" and not "How intelligent are you?" That small change makes all the difference.

v

The Influence of Teachers consists of three sections.

The chapters that make up "Follow the Teacher" are generally optimistic in tone and content. They are largely concerned with what goes on inside classrooms and schools.

Most of the chapters in "Follow the Leader" are about the education leaders I've been privileged to spend time – often years – with.

My hopes and suggestions are set forth in a final chapter.

Section One:

Follow the Teacher

1

The Influence of Teachers

After college in the mid-1960s, I spent two years as a high school English teacher at Paul D. Schreiber High School in Port Washington, N.Y. Although I've been around educators for most of my professional life, these would be the only years I taught high school full time. So it was to my great surprise when, in 2006, some former Schreiber students invited me to their 40th high school reunion. How could they possibly remember me? And how could I turn down such an opportunity? I accepted the invitation and prepared for a sentimental stroll down memory lane. What the day ended up offering, though, was altogether different: a powerful reminder of the lasting influence that teachers have on the lives of their students, as well as some insights into where education in this democratic nation has missed the mark in recent years.

Like most high schools in the 1960s, Paul D. Schreiber High School was rigidly tracked. As a new teacher fresh out of college, I wasn't allowed near the top two tracks of college-bound students, the "ones" and "twos." Instead, I was assigned to what the administration called "threes" and "fours" – students we weren't supposed to expect much from. Fortunately, I didn't have a philosophy of education or any real plan at the time. I didn't know how I was supposed to approach "those kids." So I did with my students what William Sullivan, my English teacher at the

Taft School in Connecticut during my junior and senior years, had done for me: I made my kids rewrite and rewrite again, as often as necessary, until their themes and essays were well-written and persuasive.

I hadn't learned how to be a teacher while I was in college. I'd majored in English at Dartmouth, not education. But I had an image of Mr. Sullivan in my head and, because I thought he was an effective teacher, I adopted some of his techniques. Mr. Sullivan demanded our best and didn't cut anyone any slack. He wasn't mean, but he could be caustic even as he was encouraging us. He would give what he called the "2-8-2" writing test almost daily. He'd write a phrase on the board, tell us we had two minutes to think about it, eight minutes to write, and then the final two minutes to proofread what we had written. The top grade was a 10, but any significant error in spelling or punctuation meant a zero. If we were writing dialogue and wanted a character to speak in incomplete sentences, we had to mark these "sentence errors" with asterisks to let him know we knew the difference. At the end of the grading period, he threw out our lowest five or 10 scores, but that didn't lessen the pressure of each 2-8-2.

I still remember some of the phrases Mr. Sullivan used as writing prompts, like "Turn out the lights. I don't want to go home in the dark." These, he said, were the dying words of someone named William Sydney Porter. What could they mean? Was he delusional or somehow insightful? (Later he told us that Porter was better known as O. Henry.) And there was an enigmatic line – "Put out the light, and then put out the light" – that we had to wrestle with, long before we read Shakespeare's *Othello*.

So there I was at Paul D. Schreiber High School, teaching "threes" and "fours:" kids who, for the most part, didn't read poetry, didn't care about Shakespeare, and didn't want to be in English class. Truth is, I didn't want to be there either. I'd been accepted into the Peace Corps earlier that year and was heading for Kenya, but when I couldn't pass the physical, I had to find a new direction. (I'd had a spinal fusion operation right after graduation, and wore an elaborate back brace for my first semester at Schreiber.)

But I was lucky. At Schreiber, I found some very supportive colleagues, a department chair who wanted us to be successful teachers, and a treasure trove of back issues of the magazine put out by the National Council of Teachers of English, chock full of techniques and lesson plans.

So I was a Sullivan imitator for two wonderful years and then left for graduate school at Indiana University. After Indiana, I taught again, this time at a black college in the South and in a federal prison at night. Perhaps, by this time, there was a little bit of Merrow in my teaching, but most of it was still Sullivan, along with whatever I'd learned from my Schreiber colleagues.

I offer this as prologue to the Class of 1966's 40th reunion. That night, I learned that the teachers who had influenced me also influenced my students, often in very specific ways.

Throughout the evening, I met former students, found their pictures in the yearbook and asked after a while, "What's your story?" Wow, the things they told me, and the valleys and hills they described. But even the sad stories were bathed in survivor's light. As I listened, I learned a lot about myself as a teacher, as well.

The first person to come up to me, calling me Mr. Merrow even though we were both in our 60s, thanked me for helping him become a writer. "You made us rewrite everything," he said, "and later on, when I realized that I had something to say, I knew that I would be able to say it clearly, as long as I rewrote it." I asked what sort of things he wrote about. Transgender issues mostly, he said. When I started leafing through the yearbook to find his picture, he added, "I was a girl then." Sure enough, "Dana" had become "Steve."

That development would certainly have shocked Mr. Sullivan, but he would have been happy about the rewriting.

A woman came up to me and began reciting the lyrics to "Fun, Fun, Fun" by the Beach Boys. ("She's got her daddy's car, she can cruise to the hamburger stand now; she forgot all about the library, like she told her old man now.") She told me I'd taught her class poetry by starting with popular songs, and then got them to read *Renascence* by Edna St. Vincent Millay and the war poetry of Wilfred Owen. Details I didn't recall.

Another former student, who described himself as a "classic underachiever," said he'd been so angry about being forced to rewrite his term paper that he swore he'd show me by making something of himself. He's now a lawyer. Mr. Sullivan would be proud.

Did I remember, one student wanted to know, my campaign to elevate the level of bathroom graffiti? I didn't, but learned that I'd done something Mr. Sullivan might have tried under the same circumstances. My classroom was next to the boys' room (which I used, because the faculty bathroom was two corridors away), and the walls were scrawled with the usual profanities. One day in class, my former student told me, I had semiseriously encouraged the students to "upgrade the graffiti" with lines from Shakespeare, T.S. Eliot, Edna St. Vincent Millay and others. It caught on, and "To be or not to be" replaced "Schreiber Sucks." "This is the way the world ends" took the place of "Susie does it with dogs," and so on. Before long, we had bathroom walls that would have been the envy of any university town coffeehouse.

But it wasn't just my obsession with rewriting that came to light at the reunion. That night, I discovered that I'd unconsciously absorbed from Mr. Sullivan another crucial lesson about teaching: the importance of empathizing without lowering standards.

Here's what happened. Before the reunion, I'd gone through the 1966 yearbook to see how many faces and names I could remember. One face jumped out at me: a young man named Sandy, whose life, I knew, had been awful beyond belief. His divorced parents had been alcoholics. One day his mother had drowned while intoxicated, and Sandy had been ordered by a court to live with his father on a boat in the harbor. I knew that his dad, a mean drunk, regularly beat and otherwise abused him. A guidance counselor and I used to talk about how powerless we felt. I can remember looking at Sandy in class and wondering how he held his life together. Now I was hoping to find out that he had made it.

Late in the evening, as I was leaving to go home, a man standing outside said, "Mr. Merrow?" It was Sandy. He told me he'd left home immediately after graduating, had gone into the service, and was now retired and living in Arizona. He said he was driving a school bus, just to keep busy. Had I known about his family?, he asked. I told him how hard it had been not to act sympathetic and understanding and cut him some slack on assignments. But he thanked me profusely for not letting him slide, for treating him like a regular student. I know now that that's exactly how Mr. Sullivan would have treated Sandy, but it was a pleasant shock to discover that I had, unknowingly, done the right thing.

Sandy recalled how, one Sunday, I'd seen him tooling around on his motorcycle and had called out to remind him of the huge English assignment due on Monday. He told me he'd actually been working on it all that morning and was just taking a quick break, but that he went back immediately after seeing me and finished it! Once again, a reminder of the influence of teachers. And once again, an incident that I have no memory of.

He also told me about something that had just happened on his school bus. A 15-year-old girl he'd gotten to know pretty well (well enough to know that her 16th birthday was approaching) told him that she didn't really expect to celebrate that birthday. He read her tone, correctly as it turned out, as a warning sign and went to the high school and spoke to a counselor. The girl not only made it to her 16th birthday, but also got counseling and straightened out. Sandy rightly felt that he'd made his contribution. It struck me that Sandy had been able to do for that troubled girl what his guidance counselor and English teacher hadn't been able to do for him 40 years ago. The girl Sandy helped may never know what he did for her, but hearing the story reminded me, for the hundredth time that night, that we are a part of all we touch, and what seems a small and forgettable gesture or action to us may have a deep and lasting impact on another's life. In that sense, we are all teachers.

The night of the reunion I came to understand that, more than 40 years earlier, I had not accepted the administration's label ("threes" and "fours") for these kids, but had expected them to become competent writers who could be moved, and move others, by the power of words. That is what my teachers expected of me, and I could hardly do less for my own students. In truth, I didn't really know another way.

Of course, I also know from my current work in education that I had a great deal of latitude to shape my classes as I saw fit. Most teachers today don't have the freedom to do what I did. While my job was to prepare students to pass the New York State Regents Exams, we did not have a step-by-step curriculum or regular bubble tests, and I was free to innovate. Our curriculum had enough slack in it to allow me to insist upon rewriting, and more rewriting. In my work for the *NewsHour*, I spend a lot of time with teachers, some of whom have stayed in touch over the years. I remember an email message from a veteran special education teacher in Maryland, a woman I know to be dedicated and competent. She wrote that her school had failed to make what the federal No Child Left Behind law calls "Adequate Yearly Progress" for the second year in a row and, because of that, they were going to teach to the test – because if they didn't make AYP that year, the school might be shut down. She was clearly distraught by this Sophie's Choice. She wrote, "In teaching to the test, I am afraid that we are raising a nation of idiots who may be able to pass standardized assessments without being able to think. I am trying to keep focused on the fact that we are educating the citizens of our nation's future, which is not necessarily compatible with the vision of No Child Left Behind." My heart goes out to that teacher, and I am angry that we continue to put her, and many thousands like her, in that position.

The teaching mission is complex and difficult, and yet oh-so-vital. Teachers can never declare "Mission Accomplished," because they are a bridge, not an endpoint, for all the boys and girls (and men and women) who come into their lives. Their involvement doesn't begin or end at the classroom door; or once they've covered Newton and Galileo, the Hundred Years' War or the past perfect tense; or even when the semester ends. Good teachers do a lot of counseling on the run in casual interactions, and they also do a lot of listening, often in fits and starts. Good teachers let kids talk about their feelings without saying, "I know how you feel," because they know it's always about their students' experiences, not their own. They work with kids who are a mixture of self-absorption, insecurity, raging hormones and ambition. They may have to face parents who want their offspring to get into the Ivy League and have jobs they can boast about, but the teacher's job is to help students build a self, to create the entity that will be constant company for life. That's why the best teachers listen to students and draw out their thinking, but don't try to solve every problem. That's why the best teachers empathize and care deeply about students as individuals, but never lower standards or expectations.

Some teachers believe, incorrectly, that they can improve a student's self-esteem with words and other easy expressions of praise (like high grades) even though the student isn't doing the best work that he or she can. The wisest know that accomplishment is the foundation of self-esteem. Students know when they're doing their best, and they know when they're being allowed to cut corners. They may grumble that their teachers are expecting too much, but good teachers know enough not to listen to that particular complaint.

But today it's not enough for outstanding teachers to teach and listen well. Their real challenge is to consciously push students out of their comfort zones. In a way, it's a "value added" issue. Let me put it this way: In America, unless a teacher works with the poor – in urban areas, Appalachia or wherever – most of his or her students are sufficiently well-off children of the richest society the world has ever known. What can and should teachers do to ensure that the talents and gifts they work to maximize in their already privileged students are put to use in the service of others?

It's not enough to equip these students to do well. These students need to learn to do *good*: to contribute to society, to serve. H. G. Wells observed that civilization is a race between education and catastrophe. Right now, catastrophe seems to be in the lead – and perhaps pulling away. In our current education system, the United States is suffering from a kind of bipolar disorder. We have, increasingly, two worlds: the comfortable, often smug world of wealthy (or suburban or upper-middle-class) schools, and the under-funded and inefficient schools in which the poor are isolated. Schools for the poor are most often dreary institutions with heavy emphasis on repetitive instruction and machine-scored bubble tests. Although some underprivileged schools are vibrant places of innovation and discovery, even that is not necessarily a cause for celebration; what it often means is

22

that reformers get to experiment on the poor, who lack the political clout to control their own schools or reject the do-gooders. In terms of our public education system, while we do have some wonderful schools, the trend lines are depressing.

Why expect teachers to do this work? First, because they can. Teachers are uniquely positioned, as I learned at the reunion, to make a lasting impression on hundreds of children. All they need is enough professional support and guidance on the one hand, and enough leeway on the other, to make lasting connections. And, secondly, because no one else seems willing to accept the challenge today.

In truth, I fear for our country – something I never expected to happen. I see a nation that remains fragmented. Cynicism ("All politicians are crooked"), indifference ("I don't care who wins the election") and a frightening willingness to accept authority blindly (religious fundamentalism) are on the rise, along with a growing gap between rich and poor. In Washington today, bipartisanship is nowhere to be found, and the strident voices (the Tea Party movement, for example) grow louder.

When that bleak mood strikes, I turn in one of two directions. If it's three o'clock in the morning – the time it always is in "the dark night of the soul," according to F. Scott Fitzgerald – I turn to the "self" that my teachers and parents helped me build. Living in my heart and mind, as part of that self, are the likes of John Keats, Alfred, Lord Tennyson and e.e. cummings; Bach and Mozart; Ella Fitzgerald, Frank Sinatra and Dave Brubeck; Shakespeare, Mark Twain and F. Scott Fitzgerald; Picasso and Renoir. That's good company. They help get me through the moment, and I get up to try again.

Or, if it's daytime, I go to a school and feed off the energy and youthful optimism of students and the dedication of the best teachers. I regain my balance and optimism and leave rejuvenated.

23

I left that 40th high school reunion reminded of the special place that teachers occupy in the lives of children and young people – especially those who haven't had many advantages in life. Society needs to acknowledge this truth and trust teachers to do more of the character building work that is an unspoken but vital part of their mission.

2

Learning to Read

"The green pancake went swimming in the lake and ate a fish."

When the first-graders in Elizabeth Holloway's class read that nonsensical sentence on the blackboard, they almost jumped out of their chairs, waving their hands excitedly.

"Is something wrong with that story?" I asked.

"Lots!" they shouted, volunteering that pancakes weren't green, can't swim and don't eat fish.

That silly story, or some variation of it, produced similar reactions in another first-grade class at Benjamin Banneker Elementary School in New Orleans and in first-grade classes at Fannie C. Williams Elementary School, also in New Orleans. That is, the children - virtually all low-income, high-poverty African Americans - read what I wrote and understood what they were reading.

To be doubly certain, I then picked children at random and asked them to read from *Nate the Great*, a book that's not used in New Orleans first-grade classes. All the children in all four classrooms read with comprehension.

Learning to read with understanding is the foundation for all learning, but most low-income children in the United States are below grade level in reading by fourth grade. So *every*

New Orleans first-grader who learns to read in school is beating the odds.

In the years *before* Hurricane Katrina, most New Orleans public school first-graders were not learning to read. In 2008, only 26 percent of eighth-graders read with proficiency, and 85 percent of all students were 18 months or more behind.

Long before Katrina, parents of school-age children had voted with their checkbooks; in 2005, more than half of New Orleans children were in private or parochial schools.

After Katrina, Louisiana created the Recovery School District to run 60 of the city's worst schools and in 2007 hired Paul Vallas, who had run the Chicago and Philadelphia school systems with some success. Vallas filled 30 percent of his classrooms with teachers from Teach For America, TeachNOLA and Troops for Teachers, programs that recruit eager but untrained people and give them summer training before they begin teaching.

New Orleans has made progress. On the spring 2008 state tests, students in grades 3-12 made gains at nearly every level in math and reading. However, most students remained below grade level. "I tell people that we're at base camp preparing to climb Mount Everest, but last year we weren't even in the Himalayas," Vallas said.

However, unless *first-graders* are learning to read, New Orleans will be playing catch-up forever.

Benjamin Banneker, where Elizabeth Holloway was teaching, is one of a handful of schools not devastated by Katrina and the flooding. Banneker, which sits on a piece of high ground called "the sliver by the river," enrolls 464 students in grades pre-K-8, and 94 percent of its students receive free or reduced-price lunch, a generally accepted marker for poverty.

Fannie C. Williams Elementary School (489 students, 93 percent receiving free or reduced-price lunches) was nothing more than a collection of trailers, way out in east New Orleans, when I visited. Most of that part of the city was under water for weeks, rendering nearly all school buildings unusable. When I was there, Williams had no playground to speak of – but I did meet the school's experienced principal, Kelly Batiste.

Banneker's principal, Cherylynn Branche, has staffed her school with veteran teachers. "I prefer people who know what they're doing," she said. "I prefer people who have a proven track record. I prefer people who are going to stay here and work with our children for the long haul." By contrast, 40 percent of Batiste's classroom teachers when I visited were new, many from Teach For America or a similar organization.

But experience may not be the key variable. Second-graders in Lindsay Enters' class were reading with excitement and comprehension. The University of Wisconsin graduate was part of TeachNOLA. "There is really no way to prepare yourself for teaching and the challenges you face," she said in 2008. "It's the same for people coming out of regular education programs." The rookie teacher decided to make reading the core of her class, "to make them all phenomenal readers," she said. "When I came in not one of them was reading their chapter books and now I have 16 out of 19 doing it."

She said she understood that not everyone could teach a child to read and admitted that she approached the task with some trepidation. "Reading is something that always frightened me a little bit, because it is such a responsibility. I don't know that everyone could teach reading. To be a teacher you need to be able to assess where the children are, and know where you're headed."

Then she said what for me are the magic words: "If I'm teaching it, but they aren't getting it, then I have to change what I'm doing." In other words, if the kids aren't learning, the teacher has to do something different. Attitude matters!

Of course, not all New Orleans first-graders are reading. Sarah T. Reed Elementary (553 students, 94 percent receiving free or reduced-price lunches) was also a collection of trailers in east New Orleans when I visited. As at Banneker and Williams, the majority of Reed students live in poverty, but the similarities seemed to end there at the time of my visit. My nonsense story about the pancake produced a less enthusiastic response, and fewer hands went in the air when I asked what was wrong with the story.

Only one or two children were able to read from *Nate the Great* with comprehension. Most read without expression – clear evidence that they did not understand the meaning. One boy, already 8, could not even decode.

If there's a silver lining anywhere in these bleak results, it seems to have taken a perfect storm of inauspicious circumstances at Reed to create the disaster. When I visited Reed in 2008, the principal and 75 percent of her teachers were in their first year. The school expected 125 students, but 387 showed up. One first-grade class was taught by a substitute from January to June because the regular teacher was let go for reasons the principal wouldn't explain. How close to the bottom of the barrel was she scraping? Whenever I looked in on his class during the day, the sub was wearing a Bluetooth device; at least twice he appeared to be engaged in telephone conversations.

Another first-grade teacher, a military veteran hired in November 2008, acknowledged her lack of preparation at the time. "I didn't think I could teach the children to read," said Nicole Tate. "I thought, 'Maybe if I let them read and they hear themselves read, they'll be better readers.' But I never had anybody say, 'Okay Miss Tate, you're doing this wrong, but let me show you how to do it.' Nobody never [sic] came, so I had to figure it out on my own."

Principal Daphyne Burnett said she'd asked for more help but was given only one "reading interventionist."

What might the future hold for Reed's many non-readers, or for other children who don't master reading in first-grade? Research indicates that children who are behind in reading in first grade have only a 1-in-8 chance of catching up. But if New Orleans devotes serious resources to the school, including well-trained veterans and more "interventionists," the grim prognosis could be reversed.

However, those children do *not* need more drill in decoding. Reading specialists often draw a false distinction between decoding and comprehending, and because most tests reward decoding, teachers in the early grades may be tempted to treat it as a goal rather than what it is: a means to an end.

It's also high time to stop fighting the Reading Wars. Children are the only casualties of this protracted standoff between crusaders for phonics and defenders of whole language. That this battle continues to rage is a perfect example of systems putting adult interests – money and ego – ahead of those of children.

A dozen years ago I tracked the progress of a classroom of first-graders, as their first-year teacher tried to teach them to read. Employing the method known as whole language, she taught the children to recognize words. Using the same book for months at a time, she convinced the children – and perhaps herself – that they were learning to read. Only at the end of the year when I asked the children, all African-American and low-income, to read from a book they had never seen did they realize that they had not been taught to read.

The painful irony of that situation was that, on the first day of school, the teacher had asked the children what they wanted to achieve that year. While a few wanted to get to know their fathers or go see a grandparent, the majority told her that they wanted to learn to read!

Across the hall, the first-graders in veteran Johnny Brinson's class learned to read with comprehension. No ideologue, Brinson used a combination of techniques – "whatever works," he told me. He taught his kids that letters have sounds associated with them, and that the sounds change depending on the combinations of letters. He teased and cajoled, scolded and praised, but he never seemed to lower his expectations or standards in the 20 or more days that I spent in his class during the year. The rookie matched Mr. Brinson when it came to affection; her problem was that no one had taught her how to teach reading.

The national goal, all children reading by the end of *third* grade, is a low floor that I fear may become a ceiling in many schools. Children don't learn to walk just so they can walk in place; they want to be able to get somewhere more efficiently. So too with reading; children want to learn to read so they can make sense of the world around them. Good teachers capitalize on that intrinsic motivation and teach children the many strategies they need to read with understanding, of which decoding is only a part.

What is happening in New Orleans should *not* stay in New Orleans. Principals everywhere should put their best teachers in first grade and kindergarten and then devote whatever additional resources are needed to ensure that children learn to read with comprehension. To do otherwise is to create candidates for remediation, special education and other expensive programs.

3

Learning to Teach

To what extent is classroom teaching a skill? How long does it take to learn those skills, and is there a best way to learn them? These are important questions at any time, but I submit they are of particular importance today, with Teach For America (and other alternative routes into the classroom) in ascendance.

There's no doubt about Teach For America's ascendancy. What began in 1990 with 500 men and women working in six communities had about 7,300 Teach For America corps members working in 35 high-poverty urban and rural areas in school year 2010-11, teaching nearly half a million children. In its first 20 years it put a total of more than 14,000 teachers into hard-to-staff schools, usually for two-year stints.

And it's about to grow even larger. In mid-2010 TFA received $50 million from the federal government's so-called i3 "Invest in Innovation" grant fund. It plans to use that money, and the required match, to nearly double its teaching corps from 7,300 teachers now to 13,000 teachers in 52 sites within five years.

During the 2008 presidential campaign, both candidates spoke favorably about the program. President Obama continues to speak highly of it. For example, when he signed the Edward M. Kennedy Serve America Act in April 2009, he cited the growing popularity of TFA as evidence of young America's

31

commitment to public service, saying in part: "I've seen a rising generation of young people work and volunteer and turn out in record numbers ... they have become a generation of activists possessed with that most American of ideas – that people who love their country can change it ... they are why 35,000 young people applied for only 4,000 slots in Teach For America."

That's a 42 percent increase over the previous year, and many of those young people come straight out of our finest colleges and universities.

And when I linked President Obama and TFA in a Google search, it produced nearly 9 million citations.

At his Senate confirmation hearing in January 2009, Obama's choice for secretary of education, Arne Duncan, had high praise for Teach For America and for Wendy Kopp herself.

Teach For America has become a household word in its short history. I suspect everyone knows that Kopp developed the idea as her senior thesis at Princeton in 1989 and then founded the program in 1990. Although only about a quarter of those who serve remain in the classroom beyond two years, over 60 percent of TFA "graduates" stay connected to public education. Prominent alumni include KIPP founders Mike Feinberg and Dave Levin and former D.C. Chancellor Michelle Rhee.

In a funny way, I was *in* Teach For America long before Wendy Kopp came up with the idea. I had been accepted into the Peace Corps and was scheduled to teach English in East Africa, before I failed the physical just a few months prior to graduation from Dartmouth in 1964. Even though I'd taken only one education course in college, I was determined to teach. And so, two months after my spinal fusion and still in a brace, I began teaching at Schreiber.

I worked long hours, spent most weekends grading papers, made a lot of mistakes and tried to bring imagination and creativity into my lessons. There were four other rookies on the staff that year. We supported each other, and, to be truthful, we shared a certain smug attitude toward many of the veteran teachers, who we felt were just putting in the hours and didn't care as much about the kids as we did.

By the end of my second year, I hit my stride and was, I believe, doing a pretty good job. That's when I left to go to graduate school.

As a reporter, I've been in a fair number of classrooms with TFA corps members. On our website you'll find a series of video portraits of Teach For America teachers at work, with scenes from their classrooms in New Orleans high schools. I think you will end up liking all of these young men and women. We certainly did. And you would be thrilled to have some of them teaching your children, but probably not all of them.

A careful viewer of our *Teaching for America* series detected a thread running through many of the TFA teacher profiles. "Most of these teachers seem to be overly concerned about control," he told me. "I get the feeling that they've been taught some simple rule like 'Control first, teaching next.'"

"What about Lindsay or Colleston?" I asked him, referring to the two most successful TFA teachers.

"They're the exception," he said. "They seem to understand that control is a by-product of stimulating education."

I told the man about a Teach For America rookie whose class we visited in early February 2010. Matt Taylor was teaching English at an alternative school, a middle school for kids who are four, five or six years below grade level. Just imagine trying to teach 16-year-olds whose literacy level is not much above *See Spot Run,* but who are acutely sensitive to their age/skill level discrepancy. In the 90-minute class I observed, Matt engaged his students in eight or nine different activities, using a Promethean Board to make everything interactive. He peppered students with questions, rewarding correct answers without calling attention to incorrect ones. At one point he displayed a long paragraph on the board – a passage that contained at least a dozen errors in grammar, spelling and punctuation. What ensued was a game in which all but one student engaged (one slept most of the class). If I remember correctly, Matt told the students that he had found only 12 errors. They found two or three more and enjoyed the triumph of outdoing their teacher, a darn good strategy on the teacher's part.

Control was not an issue, ever. It never is when kids are engaged.

In my experience, Teach For America corps members are almost always fun to be around, because they are bright, energetic and outgoing. Their idealism and goodness virtually ooze out of every pore. What's not to like?

Well, to be honest, sometimes their *teaching* is not to like. After all, they are first-year teachers who have had just five or six weeks of summer training and a short orientation in their assigned cities. They make all sorts of rookie mistakes. Occasionally I recognized in them that smug attitude I once exhibited toward veterans.

It's a curious paradox that teaching, the profession that is *easiest* to get into, can be, at the same time, among the most difficult to enter. Most schools of education accept just about everyone who applies, but Teach For America, which puts all those capable, smart, idealistic young men and women into some of the country's toughest public schools, rejects an astonishing number (88 percent last year) of its applicants. At more than 20 colleges and universities, Teach For America was the top recruiter. At Harvard, 13 percent of graduating seniors applied. At Spelman College in Atlanta, 25 percent did. If they don't make the cut at TFA, many will then fall back to their *second* choices, often a top law or business school.

Nearly all – 78 percent – of those accepted will enter TFA. By contrast, only about 70 percent of those accepted into Yale chose to enroll.

What I find most impressive about Teach For America is how it continues to work to improve the model. In 2010 it released the results of an intensive study of its most successful teachers. What was it about them, TFA hoped to find out, that made them successful? And could TFA fine-tune its own admission process to make sure it accepted more who had those qualities? In a highly readable and thoughtful article in *The Atlantic*, Steven Farr, Teach For America's chief knowledge officer, told writer Amanda Ripley, "Great teachers constantly reevaluate what they are doing." He added: "Superstar teachers had four other tendencies in common: they avidly recruited students and their families into the process; they maintained focus, ensuring that everything they did contributed to student learning; they planned exhaustively and purposefully – for the next day or the year ahead – by working backward from the desired outcome; and they worked relentlessly, refusing to surrender to the combined menaces of poverty, bureaucracy, and budgetary shortfalls."

It may well be that Teach For America's greatest contribution to education will not be the kids who are helped or the talented young men and women who develop a connection with and affection for public education, but its relentless self-examination – a process that quite simply puts the rest of teacher education to shame. If Teach For America can work hard to figure out why some of its trainees become better teachers than others, why can't regular schools of education?

One reason they don't is that many schools of education accept just about everyone who applies. The implication of being able to predict the likelihood of an applicant's becoming a successful teacher based on his or her application is that some applicants would be denied admission. TFA wants to be in that position, but do most schools of education? "Asked and answered," as the lawyers say.

The national accrediting body for teacher education, NCATE, has finally responded to the challenge. Its November 2010 report, "Transforming Teacher Education through Clinical Practice," begins with the bold assertion that "The education of teachers in the United States needs to be turned upside down," a statement few will disagree with. It goes on: "To prepare effective teachers for 21st century classrooms, teacher education must shift away from a norm which emphasizes academic preparation and course work loosely linked to school-based experiences. Rather, it must move to programs that are fully grounded in clinical practice and interwoven with academic content and professional courses." The blue-ribbon panel says that those who intend to teach should spend more time in schools (but what about those who teach the teachers?). It calls for close cooperation with school districts, shared responsibility for outcomes, and tougher admission standards for would-be teachers.

And, in a departure from the past, this report says that the institutions that do the training should be held accountable for whether kids taught by their graduates are learning: "All teacher education programs should be accountable for–and their accreditation contingent upon – how well they address the needs of schools and help improve P-12 student learning."

Peppered throughout the report are encouraging phrases like "fundamentally redesign" and "significant changes," but the panel wants some changes that will be difficult, if not impossible, to bring about. It wants universities to make sure that education departments get their fair share of resources, because clinical-based training is more expensive than the current classroom-based approach. It wants schools of education to raise their admission standards, but I suspect that's something they would have done a long time ago if they could have. And finally, it wants education professors to stop lecturing from yellowed notes and model what they are now going to be preaching—good luck with that one!

Eight states, including California and Colorado, have agreed to pilot the recommendations.

By rights, Wendy Kopp and her TFA colleagues should be opening a bottle of champagne.

The success of TFA inspired the Jack Kent Cooke Foundation to create an equivalent program that provides guidance and counseling to encourage low-income high school and community college students to earn their bachelor's degrees; it's awarded 11 $1 million grants to date. The program recruits and trains recent college graduates from top colleges and universities to work as full-time advisors for a year or two after graduation. "It will be the next Teach For America," Vance Lancaster, formerly of the Foundation, wrote in an email in 2008, although they're not calling it "Advise For America." Instead it's the "College Advising Corps."

But I believe that the success of Teach For America reveals an unpleasant truth about how *little* we value education and children. Consider nursing – another helping profession that's often compared with teaching. Just as there's a teaching shortage, the United States desperately needs nurses. Hospitals today have more than 135,000 empty nursing slots, according to the American Association of Colleges of Nursing.

But there is no "Nurse For America" program, because it's *inconceivable* that someone could step in and provide nursing care after just five weeks of summer training.

Just imagine: "Hi, Mrs. Lingering. I'm John Merrow, your new nurse. I just graduated from Dartmouth. Now let's see … it says you get two cc's of this medicine. That's about the same as a tablespoon, isn't it? And I'm supposed to examine you. I'm pretty sure I remember which orifice this instrument goes in."

No, we will never have a "Nurse For America" program, because that profession's standards are higher than those of teaching. Nobody says, "Those who can, do. Those who can't, *nurse*." That slur is reserved for teaching, an occupation that's ridiculously easy to join.

So, two-and-a-half cheers for Teach For America, but wouldn't it be wonderful if "Nurse For America" and TFA were *equally* inconceivable? If teaching could become not merely an honorable calling but also a well paid, well-respected profession that's difficult to get into?

4

Serious Fun?

The shrill whistle pierced the humid August air, and the 10 players – all African-American high school students – gathered around the referee. The ref pointed to a young man wearing a T-shirt.

"Malik, here's the word. 'Ambiguous.' Define it and use it in a sentence." The young man did so in a strong voice, and the ref called over to the scorer's desk, "That's a point for the Shirts!"

Then he turned to the other team (the Skins), picked out a player, and gave him a word: "Optimism." When the player confused the noun with the adjective, the ref turned to a player on the Shirts, who gave the correct answer.

"Another point for the Shirts," the ref called. "Now let's play ball!"

At least a dozen times during that game the ref, a 30-something English teacher named David Felsen, stopped play for vocabulary. As I recall, the "vocabulary points" amassed by the Shirts provided the margin of victory.

I say 'as I recall' because that game took place more than 25 years ago on a basketball court at a Friends School in Philadelphia. David Felsen, the man who created that program, went on to become headmaster of the school. When he left to lead another school, the summer games continued – as they do even now. The rules for Felsen's summer program were simple: Do the reading and other homework if you want to play basketball. Skip the homework, and you sit out the game. Define the words correctly, and your team gets points. Over the years the intervention worked: Dozens and dozens of young African-American boys from inner-city Philadelphia went on to college – perhaps with basketball scholarships, perhaps not.

That program's genius was that it met kids where they were. In this case, they were mad for basketball. It recognized that kids love to play and compete. They'll study in order to get on the court, and, once on the court, they'll do their best to "score" by knowing the words. Nobody wants to be embarrassed publicly or let the team down. Moreover, the rewards were immediate: no waiting around for the results of machine-scored tests.

Children learn valuable lessons – and not just vocabulary or math – by playing games. A seventh-grader who was playing on an organized team for the first time told me about her team's success: "It's like our team did really good so far this season and we're just getting ready for the championship. Now, we want to win it, so we still know we have a lot of work to do and it's not been easy getting here, but it feels really good, and I think it feels really good because we know we have actually worked together to do this."

The best games teach teamwork and cooperation. Children like that seventh-grader learn that their chances of winning improve when they work together. Play is natural, but children also seem to know intuitively that play is serious fun.

When I posted a version of this on my blog in mid-2009, a teacher named Steve Peha weighed in. School has to be fun, he said, but it can't be fake fun, like an occasional game. "Fun can't be icing on the cake," he said. "It has to be baked in. What's not fun? Using a textbook. Doing test-prep activities. Having no choices over what you study. Being told again and again that

40

you're a bad student because you keep getting D's and F's, even though the problem is the material you're studying – it's way above your grade level and there's no differentiated instruction going on."

Systems seem to lose sight of a basic truth: Learning, a natural human experience, *is* inherently fun. We are a curious species. As the Nobel Prize-winning physicist Leon Lederman told us, all children are instinctive natural scientists, and schools and teachers have to learn to get out of the way. Nurture, don't kill, their desire to learn.

Mr. Peha elaborated on this idea: "It's the traditions of school that take the fun out of learning. It's the mindless focus on product over process and participation. It's discovering that school is not about you. It's teachers who have forgotten that teaching is fun who take the fun out of learning."

Sneaking education into summer games is one thing, but can games, and the spirit of games, be made essential to education in genuine system-changing ways? Can schools meet kids where they are and devise ways to take them to places that we, as adults, know they need to be?

Bringing games and competition into classes with spelling bees and math Olympiads works, but in my experience many teachers trivialize games and score-keeping by giving points for good behavior and taking away points for misdeeds. Texas pioneered "No Pass, No Play" rules, setting an academic bar for varsity sports, but that's working from the negative. And a lot of what happens now in schools is basically a 'gotcha' game, in which deficiencies and shortcomings are identified.

One word that educators are overly fond of reveals their thinking. That word is 'rigor,' something they demand and/or celebrate. But as Debbie Meier pointed out a long time ago, the word connotes harsh, unyielding behavior. Think 'rigor mortis.'

Swear off 'rigor' and 'rigorous,' and substitute 'challenging' instead.

Have we forgotten that kids are people, too? That they enjoy what we all enjoy: the thrill of independence coupled with meaningful, healthy social interaction with others, the opportunity to know they are learning, to be able to monitor their own progress, and meaningful work that is neither too easy nor impossibly hard?

Here's why I worry. I hear educators talking all the time about "getting kids *ready to learn.*" Well, do'h! Kids are *born* ready to learn. We are a curious species by nature. Who are these educators who don't get that, and why are they still holding sway over our children? Either re-educate them, or get them out, and maybe we can move ahead.

Can school be serious fun? Should it be? If so, how? We need rules, a way to keep score, a referee, reasonably high stakes, genuine results, meaningful competition, teamwork – and *fun*.

As I argued in the preface to this volume, schools must become places where young people are encouraged to ask questions, not simply regurgitate answers. Schools must be intellectually safe places where it's okay *not* to know everything. What I am calling 'Intellectual Safety' is a critical issue in schools; without it, children are left vulnerable to cruelty and torment in the very place that they're supposed to feel safe enough to open their minds and learn. School's no fun, for sure.

"There can't be a climate where the kids laugh at the wrong answer," Ted Sizer, the late and beloved school reformer, once told me. "When that happens, a kid will immediately shut down and refuse to participate. And that's when learning stops. For me, the ultimate test of a school is the willingness of any student to display his or her ignorance, because the riskiest thing you can do in a school, whatever your age, is to say, 'I don't know' or 'I don't understand.'"

Just how common is intellectual safety in schools? "It's not as common as it should be," says E.D. Hirsch, Jr. "That's the kind of safety I'm most interested in, because it's the most closely-connected to academic achievement, which is what I think schools should be focused on."

Think about what happens in most classrooms when a student admits he doesn't understand and asks for clarification. Other students snicker and begin teasing their bewildered classmate. In excellent schools, however, a display of ignorance, coupled with a desire to understand, is applauded. That sounds like a contradiction, but as Sizer noted: "Unless a kid can say, 'I don't get it, I don't understand,' secure in the knowledge that the adults will try to fill that void, genuinely excellent education is impossible. So in a really excellent school, the kids who are struggling know that their struggle is respected as legitimate, and so they're willing to expose themselves, to be vulnerable."

Parents should take note that they can (and often do) contribute to a climate of "intellectual danger" by putting intense pressure on their children to "get it right" and earn honor grades. Pressure to achieve those external rewards creates an atmosphere in which kids are afraid to explore, afraid to take intellectual risks and afraid to say, "I don't know."

The late Frank McCourt, author of *Angela's Ashes* and *Tis*, taught English at one of New York City's elite public high schools for 18 years, an experience that brought him into daily contact with parental pressure. In his entire career at Stuyvesant, he told me, only one parent asked, "Is my son enjoying school?" McCourt was shocked. "Only one. The rest would say things like, 'Oh God, is he doing his work?' and 'I'm worried about his PSAT's and his SAT's,' and 'She hasn't finished her application to Yale and Cornell.'"

McCourt said that forced him to question what he was doing with his own life. He began to doubt the direction public education was taking. "We test and test, because we want to make sure a kid fits, but we don't pursue wisdom in any Socratic way. We ought to want to have the kids think for themselves and not to be afraid to think for themselves, but they're discouraged from doing that because they're told all the time 'the test, the test, the test.'"

Intellectual safety means more than being able to say, "I don't know." It means that students feel free to think and question and doubt. It also means being free to take unpopular positions. "Schools must encourage the idea of rational persuasion," Hirsch said. "A student might have some oddball idea like 'the Holocaust never happened.' That would then be discussible, although I would like to think that reason would prevail. It's the old Jeffersonian principle: 'We tolerate any error as long as reason is free to combat it.' I would like to feel that we encourage an atmosphere in which we didn't let a false idea go without at least an attempt at rational persuasion."

An intellectually safe school values ideas and exploration. As the educator Luyen Chou, who is also chief product officer for Schoolnet Inc., told me, "It's an environment where students do not feel restricted in their ability to admit what they don't know. And the teachers feel that they can admit that as well." In that environment, Chou says, there's a communal commitment to knowledge building, instead of classrooms where teachers present a set of facts and ideas that students must learn and regurgitate.

Intellectual safety – freedom to make mistakes and raise questions – allows real teaching and real learning to happen. As writer Alfie Kohn notes, "In excellent classrooms, the teacher is always listening, always watching, to see what kind of mistakes are being made and what information that provides me about how this kid's mind is working."

I asked Kohn for an example. "Let's say the answer to a math problem is 17 but a kid says 18. A lot of caring teachers in 'good enough' classrooms might try to be supportive and sympathetic and say, 'Ooh, you're close.' But that's silly and counterproductive, because the teacher doesn't know why the kid missed. The kid might not understand the underlying principle and just by luck arrived one digit away from the correct answer."

In Kohn's view, the excellent teacher would push to find out how the student arrived at her answer – even when the answer is correct. "The teacher shouldn't just say it when the kid's wrong, because you want to know how the student is looking at this issue. What has he gotten or failed to quite grasp that has led to his answer? When a teacher creates a climate of safety where mistakes are truly welcomed, you have a classroom where teachers understand where kids are falling short and why, and so they're in a much better position to help them."

Kohn believes that the more schools focus on competition and rewards, the less intellectually safe they become. That is, the kids who don't win the gold stars get the message, "I'm a loser." And Kohn believes that competition undermines a school's sense of community. "What competition teaches, above all, is that other people are potential obstacles to my own success. And that is a poisonous message, for winner and loser alike, because now we can't take advantage of the kind of collaboration that leads to genuine excellence for everyone."

Intellectual competition actually is both good and natural, in my view, but if students are simply competing for places on the honor roll, it can work against excellence, as Kohn observes. Competition for grades reduces student interest in knowledge for its own sake, because, as Kohn says: "If the point is to get an award, or to get a sticker, or to get an A, now I'm less interested in figuring out the problem. I'm not interested in science now; I'm interested in beating someone else."

In a highly competitive environment, Kohn maintains, students are likely to pick the easiest possible tasks, and that's counterproductive if we want kids to pick the most interesting or most challenging. "They figure, all right, the point here is not to try something a little beyond my competence; the point here is to do what I know I can succeed at, pick the shortest book or the easiest project because the point is not understanding and excellence, the point is getting an A."

Kohn would say that truly excellent schools minimize competition, or at least place community first. That's an oversimplification, in my view. I believe that the marketplace of ideas is competitive; the rewards, however, must be more complex and more thoughtful than simple letter grades or other external rewards.

Excellent schools and excellent teachers try to put that sense of purpose first, and teach to the purpose, so that students understand why they're learning something in the first place. That's a very different mentality from learning a skill or learning a piece of the curriculum in order to pass a test or receive an external reward like an A or get into college or not make your parents angry.

Cliques are often blamed for contributing to an intellectually and emotionally unsafe school environment. I asked Sizer if he felt this was the case. That all depends, he told me; in excellent high schools adults don't try to stamp out cliques, because they're part of everyday life. "All you have to do is go into a bar or a faculty room, and see the cliques of adults," he said. "There's nothing necessarily wrong with it. Every group of kids and adults will form cliques. The kids who like to play music together. The kids who like to fix cars. The thing is to make sure they're benign." That can be done by rewarding healthy, positive cliques with support and encouragement, he said. "An excellent school has cliques of kids who say, 'We don't do that here' when something bad comes up."

46

When there is such an alliance, kids know the school is theirs, and they take pride in it. In such a school, students will approach a teacher to express concern about another student, or will ask a teacher to intervene in support of a student who's being victimized. "The truly safe school really starts with this alliance, where, if there's going to be some kind of physical violence or violence to ideas (like cheating), a significant number of kids will feel their reputation will be tarnished if something happens, and they will speak out," he said.

Sizer also said he believed that schools, perhaps the most autocratic of our institutions, should be democratically run, and that high school kids should be part of the leadership. "Why shouldn't kids that age be?" he asked. He didn't argue for formal voting but instead for a collective commitment to the school. That entails conversations with students and families, asking them, "What is school for, what's good, and what isn't, and what should be done?"

"I think the kids and adults have to make the rules together," Sizer said. "Take the issue of drugs in school. Adults cannot keep drugs out of the school unless a significant percentage of kids say, 'We don't do that here.' You can't bring in enough cops and dogs. Kids are a lot smarter than dogs. You can have searches and you can only have transparent backpacks and all that, but those are desperate steps after the situation is out of control."

In excellent schools, the adults know the students in the building and approach them with respect. School is seen as a shared enterprise, with students as partners in that enterprise. Not equal partners of course, because roles and obligations are different, but students in excellent schools are not objects to be manipulated or watched.

Instead they are searchers, questioners who share in creating knowledge. Meaningful learning is serious fun.

5

Evaluating Teachers

How can you *know* that one teacher is better than another? How should teachers be evaluated? And by whom? Should teachers be judged based on how they perform in the classroom, or by how their students do on tests?

These questions are central to one of education's hot buttons, the idea that judgments about teachers – and perhaps their salaries – should be based on how much their students learn.

The emptiness of the current approach to teacher evaluation was brought into the spotlight in 2009 with the publication of "The Widget Effect," a report by the New Teacher Project. Researchers studied evaluation in 12 districts in four states, surveying 15,000 teachers and 1,300 administrators. What they learned is that *virtually every teacher is outstanding*, at least according to their evaluations. "In districts that use binary evaluation ratings (generally 'satisfactory' or 'unsatisfactory'), more than 99 percent of teachers receive the satisfactory rating. Districts that use a broader range of rating options do little better; in these districts, 94 percent of teachers receive one of the top two ratings and less than 1 percent are rated unsatisfactory."

Obviously administrators and teachers know the evaluation system is a fraud, because 81 percent of administrators and 58 percent of teachers acknowledged that their schools employed tenured teachers who weren't performing adequately.

48

And when virtually every teacher is good or great, how can a truly outstanding teacher be recognized?

So how does classroom evaluation work, according to the study? It's not pretty.

"Evaluations are short and infrequent (most are based on two or fewer classroom observations totaling 60 minutes or less), conducted by untrained administrators, and influenced by powerful cultural forces – in particular, an expectation among teachers that they will be among the vast majority rated as top performers."

I've sat in on evaluations during my reporting for the *NewsHour* and have to agree. In fact, we once produced a piece comparing a teacher's evaluation to a figure skating exhibition: carefully choreographed and well-rehearsed, with the judges sitting there knowing exactly what to expect. That metaphor nailed the artifice of teacher evaluation but missed the emptiness. In skating, the contestant can get low scores, something "The Widget Effect" suggests almost never happens in classroom evaluations.

Was classroom evaluation ever a useful process? Has the method of evaluating teachers (administrators in the back of the room watching and taking notes) ever felt collegial and professional? I decided to ask some teachers, some from "the good old days" and some who are teaching today, how frequent, and how useful, their evaluations have been. Let me start with a teacher who was never evaluated at all!

Dal Lawrence, the long-time union leader in Toledo, began as a high school history teacher. "I had the perfect evaluation. My first four semesters in Toledo, I got satisfactory evaluations four consecutive times, but I never saw a person in my classroom. That's perfect, isn't it? I went down at the end of the first year and I said to the principal, 'Ray, how do you know I'm satisfactory? You haven't been in my classroom.' He said, 'Ah-h, the kids would let me know if you weren't.'"

(Lawrence went on to develop a dramatically different approach to evaluating teachers called PAR for 'Peer Assistance and Review.' More about that later.)

Stanford professor Linda Darling-Hammond, who taught high school English in 1973-1974, was also left completely alone. "I was never observed at all during my first year, not once," she told me. My own situation was eerily similar. In my first year teaching high school English in the mid-'60s, I taught 900 classes – five classes a day for 180 days – and remember being observed only three times.

David Cohen, who teaches high school in Palo Alto, said: "In my first California public school job, over in Fremont, I was observed once or twice a year by principals with science backgrounds (I'm an English teacher). ... They saw that I controlled the classroom, but did little to engage me in questions/reflections about my instructional choices or goals for improvement."

That's how the system worked in "the good old days." You closed your door and ran things your way, and as long as your class wasn't noisy enough to bother anyone else, you were assumed to be doing your job. Administrators rarely opened classroom doors to see what was going on, and teachers watched each other at work even less frequently. (That's changing now: In some schools, teachers get to watch their peers teach, after which they share their analysis. In other schools, though, principals armed with lists sit in the back of the class checking off behaviors and later give the teachers "scorecards" with their "batting average.")

As for me, I remember being observed by my high school principal in Port Washington, N.Y. After sitting in on a lively discussion of *Macbeth*, he took me aside and suggested that if I would just remember to use the bathroom before class, I wouldn't have to move around so much!

And what about today? Most districts still require observations, with the numbers and procedures often spelled out in union contracts. These rules may be honored in the breach, of course, as in the past. But most important is whether observations are actually useful. The 2010 Scholastic/Gates Foundation survey of 40,000 teachers sheds some light on this. Here's part of that report's summary:

> Teachers are skeptical of current measures of teacher performance, with only 22% indicating that principal observation is a very accurate measure. At the same time, more than half of teachers indicate that student academic growth (60%) and student engagement (55%) are very accurate measures of teacher performance—much more so than teacher tenure, which a significant number of teachers said is not at all accurate. When asked about teacher retention, nearly all teachers say that non-monetary rewards like supportive leadership and collaborative working environments are the most important factors to retaining good teachers. Fewer than half of teachers say higher salaries are absolutely essential for retaining good teachers and only 8% say pay for performance is absolutely essential.

My own non-scientific sample suggests that, although the process may be changing for the better in some places, it is, unfortunately, still mostly useless.

Chris Krook-Magnuson, who began teaching math at Coolidge High School in Washington, D.C., in 2005 said: "I was observed two times by an administrator my first year and did not receive useful feedback, just a checklist of what I was supposed to have posted in the room and on the board. I was supposed to be observed by my American University Mentor (as part of my M.A.T.), but I never saw her that entire year."

Teachers watching teachers doesn't happen very often, according to the 2009 MetLife Survey of the American Teacher. It reports: "The least frequent type of collaborative activity is teachers observing each other in the classroom and providing feedback. Less than one-third of teachers or principals report that this frequently occurs at their school."

The MetLife survey divides teachers into two groups: those who teach in schools with high and low levels of collaboration. The results suggest that the answer to that age-old question "What do teachers want?" is *collaboration*. Forty-five percent of teachers in "high-collaboration" schools get to observe each other teach, versus 10 percent in the "low-collaboration" schools. Similar results run though the survey. In the "high" schools, 95 percent of new teachers get to work with experienced colleagues, versus 59 percent in "low" schools. In the "high" schools, 95 percent of teachers say their principal pays attention to their views about school improvement strategies, versus 48 percent in "low" schools. And 94 percent of "high-collaboration" schools have structured time for teachers to meet, versus only 47 percent of "low-collaboration" schools.

Because much learning – including when teachers are doing the learning – is social, veteran educator Ann Lieberman told me, "teacher evaluation shouldn't be about finding fault but about helping teachers learn by building on what they already know, what can help them move forward, and what can help them become more thoughtful about the complexities of their classrooms." In other words, beware of simple, simplistic approaches to evaluating teachers.

One alternative to the 'sink or swim' approach has been under our noses all along, since 1981. That's when the Toledo school district adopted PAR, the Peer Assistance and Review program. In this system, trained expert teachers mentor rookies throughout their first year. They spend at least several days every month in the new teacher's classroom and then meet to pass along advice and suggestions. At year's end, it's the job of this 'consulting teacher' to report to a 9-person council *on* the rookie's progress or lack thereof. The council (five teachers and four administrators) then votes whether to give the rookie a contract for a second year. At least six votes are required to either rehire or fire, and over the past thirty years an average of 8 percent of new teachers have been let go. Those who are rehired have had the advantage of a year of mentoring, a far cry from the usual 'sink or swim' approach that most rookie teachers experience.

One parent described PAR as a 'security blanket.' "These teachers have just graduated from college. The universities aren't paid to find out if they're a good teacher or a bad teacher, so they get into our system. They're hired and they're newly graduated teachers. And are they really competent? This allows the public schools to find out if they really are competent to teach our students. And as a parent, that's a security blanket for me."

Data indicates that PAR works. Since its inception, almost 500 first year teachers have been fired. Those who are rehired have had the benefit of a year of mentoring. No 'sink or swim' experience for them. Moreover, they have learned an additional important lesson: It's perfectly normal to need help in becoming a better teacher. They are *not* alone.

Sarah Kirkbride-Hurley, now in her 4th year of teaching, welcomed the mentoring. "When somebody sits in the back of your class and you can think about 'That person's here to help me.' Or you can think, 'That person's here to judge me.' So I chose to think 'That person's here to help me.' I think collaborating is great... If somebody else already did it really well, you should help me figure out how to do it really well too, so I don't sit there and try to figure it out myself."

The habit of collaboration has carried over, she told us. She's not at all reluctant to ask other teachers for advice and suggestions. She learned that teaching is a team sport, an unintended consequence of the PAR approach.

PAR, usually called The Toledo Plan, was the brainchild of Dal Lawrence, long time President of the Toledo Federation of Teachers. He began pitching the idea to the School Board in 1973 but was turned down because, as he recalls, evaluation was the administrators' job, not something that teachers did. It was all about turf, and schools are the epitome of 'command and control.'

But 1981 was different. Toledo had weathered a tough teachers' strike 18 months earlier and had a new Superintendent. He sent the Board's attorney to negotiate with Lawrence:

> It was the first time I ever sat across the table from another professional. And he asked me, 'Why don't my people want to do this?'
> And I said, 'Well, it's a turf issue.'
> He said, 'Well, we don't fire any teachers for bad practice, do we?'
> And I said, 'No, never.'
> So he said, 'Well, I'll get back to you.'
> And I thought, 'Yeah, right,' but he did. He came back the next session. And he got his ... pad and pencil and he said, 'All right, we're going to do this. But you're going to have to do something for us.' (And I thought, uh oh, the dreaded quid pro quo.) And he said, 'If we can use these expert teachers to also work with the *senior* teachers who are having serious problems, you got a deal.'

That would change the dynamic completely, because veteran tenured teachers were all but untouchable. Here the Board's attorney was asking for a way of reviewing their effectiveness. As Dal said, "I remember sitting there thinking, 'Eight years of trying to get this thing adopted, but we never talked to our members about senior teachers, just first year teachers.' And I thought, 'Well, I've had a lot of jobs that had less stress and more money than this one.' I stuck my hand across the table. We shook."

Dal Lawrence could be forgiven if more than his hand kept on shaking, because he then had to take this plan to his members for their vote, yea or nay. At one point, Lawrence recalled, "This teacher stood up and she said, 'Mr. Lawrence, when is this union going to start demanding that people who are not carrying their weight begin to carry their weight?' And she got an ovation. And I'm thinking, 'Wait a minute. Am I missing something here?' And when they voted, they ratified it. I don't think there was a no vote in the whole auditorium that day."

Dal Lawrence and his wife, Fran, the current President of the TFT, believe that teachers want to be part of a profession that takes responsibility for its members' performance. "Teachers don't have a vested interest in incompetence," Fran Lawrence says. "I don't know any teacher who wants to teach next door to a teacher who is not competent and who is failing their students."

Adds Dal, "Teachers, if they have the opportunity and the responsibility for competence and performance standards, they'll take that responsibility and they'll do a terrific job with it. And it's because they do want to be part of a real profession with real responsibilities." It's a matter of ownership, the Lawrences believe. Under PAR, teachers own an important part of the school's business. "What could be more important than the quality of the work of the people in the classroom," Dal Lawrence asks, rhetorically? "And that's what they own."

Fran Lawrence chimes in. "And it invests classroom teachers in the process, like other professions. The teachers influence instruction and school policy and school improvement initiatives, and when they're influencing those things, they're willing to say, 'I feel ownership and I'm willing to assume accountability for results.'"

Ownership is the key, Dal Lawrence says; "As long as you allow the old system with the boss or the foreman mentality, the teachers will step back and say, 'Well, I'm not really responsible here.' And that's bad."

Adds Fran Lawrence: "It's teachers taking ownership for standards and enforcement. And feeling that sense of community, which is what the real profession is all about. When teachers are excluded from that, or excluded from real influence over curriculum and instruction and school policy, then it's so easy (for them) to say, 'Well, you know, it's the principal's problem.'"

Lawrence's union in Toledo is part of the American Federation of Teachers, ruled then by the legendary Albert Shanker. For a time, Lawrence kept PAR under the radar, by agreement with the Board's attorney, but in 1982 Lawrence got a call. As he told me:

> 'Al would like you to come to Washington and explain what you're doing,' a secretary said. Which didn't sound exactly like a friendly invitation. I had never even shaken Al Shanker's hand. Knew who he was, of course. And so I attended my first executive council meeting.
>
> Shanker's up in front, and they're mostly elected union presidents from around the country. And we sort of rehearsed what we were going to say, and I thought, 'This is not going to be a good experience.' And Shanker said, 'Now I've invited some colleagues we have in Toledo who doing things a little different with evaluation, and I thought you ought to know about them.'
>
> With that, he turned to me and said, 'Dal' as if he had known me forever, and I got up, and my first rehearsed words were, 'We're not here to sell you anything. We're just here to tell you what we're doing,' and I did it in about seven or eight minutes, and it was bedlam. I mean, it was worse than you could possibly imagine. There was cursing, swearing, shouting ... 'Who gave those people permission to do this? It's against AFT policy. The hell with them.' And all those kinds of things.
>
> And Shanker stepped forward and he got them quieted down. He said, 'I think there's something you're missing here.' And that's the first time we knew Al Shanker was on our side. And then he started to talk about Belgium and how teachers relate to the governmental system and everything else in Belgium. And he went to Germany

and Great Britain and Australia, always juxtaposing how teachers in
America are treated. Whew!
Boy, they left that session a solemn bunch of people, and Al came
over and he shook our hand and said, 'Keep on doing it. Keep on doing it. I like what you're doing.'

Dal Lawrence professes to have been unaware of what
he was creating. "I didn't know we were doing 'peer review.' I
was just looking at medicine and how you become a doctor and
how you become a teacher and realizing that we were just so
casual about the process. No wonder we weren't respected."
What about the wrinkle added by Toledo's superintendent back in 1981 - that PAR be used to review *veteran*
teachers? Fran Lawrence maintains that it is working. "When a
teacher is placed in intervention, the union and the district are
essentially saying, 'We're going to give you the best professional
help possible,' an accomplished peer to mentor you and coach
you. Over time, if you're not able to bring your practice into an
acceptable range, you will no longer be teaching in Toledo."
But the numbers suggest a different interpretation. While
8 percent of first-year teachers are not retained, less than one half
of one percent of veteran teachers has been removed. Just 15 in
the past six years, in a teaching force of about 2,000. The 'company line' about this information is two-part: the low number
proves that PAR works because Toledo removed the ineffective
ones early; and, two, the system's way of providing help - short of
the dreaded 'intervention' - is effective. There are other forms of
assistance, but it's impossible to assess the second claim without
knowing how many veteran teachers either ask for or are given
some form of interim help.
We do know that principals are not allowed to visit classrooms for purposes of evaluation without the consent of the
teacher, a seemingly bizarre abdication of authority. Principals
can 'drop in' but they aren't allowed to 'evaluate,' a distinction I

cannot wrap my mind around. How could a principal drop in and watch a teacher at work without also 'evaluating' what's going on?

The Lawrences have an explanation, which goes something like this: Teachers are taking responsibility for their peers, and to let principals drop in and evaluate at any time would be returning to the old 'command and control' system that we have discarded.

When I was in Toledo, I sensed a general reluctance to intervene with veteran teachers and heard stories about veterans who, if faced with the possibility of intervention, immediately hired a lawyer or refused to communicate with administrators or the consulting teacher.

It's not difficult to find critics. One parent told us it all came down to money and coziness.

> PARENT: People don't like to hear that. But it's true. If you have a system where you have unions and teachers policing each other and no outside policing, then Billy can say, 'Hey, Tom, you did a good job,' and Tom can respond, 'Hey, Billy, you did a good job.' And there are no interchanges that occur.
> ME: And that doesn't work?
> PARENT: No, I don't think that works. I don't think that works in any system. If I had a system in my house where I could evaluate myself on how I clean, my evaluations would be A+, honors, cum laude.
> ME: And your house would be dirty?
> PARENT (laughs): You bet! But if I had somebody coming in and saying, 'Hey, you need to do this,' my house would be clean.

Fran Lawrence denies the system promotes coziness. "There are no barriers to identifying, or referring teachers who need help with their classroom performance, and there's no resistance," she says. "In fact, there's cooperation on the part of the union leadership."

But that same parent believes the union has too much power: "And everybody knows it, but people get blackballed. People are fearful of losing jobs. If I were to apply for a Toledo public school job and they saw this, they'd say, 'Hey, this guy, mm-m, oh, no, we're not letting him in.' And this has been going on for as long as I can remember."

At the end of the day, Dal Lawrence maintains, the PAR approach has transformed the union. Here's how he puts it: "In the old system, the union defended individuals. In the new system, the union defends standards of practice; it defends the profession." He pauses, and then adds, "Not everybody's happy with that, incidentally. But we are."

And collaboration is cheaper, Fran Lawrence says. "It's a joint effort without all of the typical confrontation. If management were going to dismiss, and we were in the role of defending, then both sides would invest huge amounts of money and legal fees, resulting in labor/management confrontation, rather than the collaboration that should happen so we can focus on student achievement."

Dal Lawrence admits that in other places unions are overly aggressive when it comes to defending ineffective teachers, but weak principals are a greater problem. "They don't do anything about it. They either ship the teacher down the street to some other unsuspecting principal, or they mark him 'Needs improvement.' And he can teach for 30 years and be marked 'needs improvement' every year until he finally retires."

Dal Lawrence's occasional lapse into evangelical enthusiasm is understandable; after all, it's his creation. As he says, "the old system, 'I'm the boss and you're not' kind of stuff, produces natural byproducts like distrust, lack of responsibility and lack of accountability. And in that system there's always somebody you can point a finger at and say, 'It's your fault.'

But when you put mechanisms in place that produce collaboration, that's a learned behavior. It produces trust and it produces accountability and responsibility as natural products. It's as simple as that."

PAR, or some variation of it, is essential for the future, Dal Lawrence believes. "The old command-and-control top down system got us to where we are," he says. "And it's not going to get out of it. It's going to make the conditions just exactly like they were yesterday, and tomorrow they're going to get worse. You got to have teamwork to build a whole new construct, a new seriousness about standards, a new seriousness about excellence and goals." Here he pauses for an instant. "And you can't leave the kids and the teachers out of that equation. It won't work."

Some form of PAR is being used by close to 100 school districts, and it's authorized in California state law. But the country has about 14,000 school districts, so PAR may not be appearing soon in your neighborhood. One obstacle, Dal Lawrence admits, are the two teacher unions. "Make no mistake about it. My wife's going to kill me for saying this, but there are people in the NEA and there are some people in AFT who don't want this stuff to succeed."

"Why?" I wanted to know.

"They're not afraid of the mentoring. They're not afraid of the evaluation. They're afraid the transformation piece. They're afraid of the new workplace culture that's evolving. They're scared to death about it." In short, they like the old command-and-control system of confrontation. They like having an enemy, he says.

But Randi Weingarten, the AFT President, says she's a fan of PAR. "I love what Toledo does," she wrote in an email in November 2010. "In fact, at the 2008 AFT convention we asked our locals to revisit the issue of peer intervention and review, and it is part of our teacher development and evaluation template."

It may take a hard slap upside the head, but unions are going to have to acknowledge what we all know – that there's a relationship between teaching and learning, and therefore student learning *must* be part of a teacher's evaluation.

Suppose a swimming instructor told the 10-year-olds in his class to swim the length of the pool to demonstrate what he'd taught them, and half of them nearly drowned in the process? Would it be reasonable to make a judgment about his effectiveness as a swimming teacher?

Or suppose that nearly all the 10-year-olds studying clarinet for the first time learned to play five or six pieces well in a semester? Would it be reasonable to consider that when deciding whether to rehire the music teacher?

Those questions answer themselves. Only an idiot would overlook student performance, be it dismal or outstanding.

However, suppose test results indicate that most students in a particular class do not have a clue about multiplying with fractions or other material in the curriculum? Should that be considered when the math teacher comes up for tenure?

Whoops, the obvious answer is wrong, because public education lives in an upside-down, irrational universe in which student outcomes have not been allowed to be connected to teaching.

Here's an excerpt from my interview with Jack Steinberg, the vice president of the teachers union in Philadelphia:

> UNION VP: You're asking can you evaluate a teacher on the performance of the students?
> ME: Yes or no?
> UNION VP: No, you cannot.
> ME (incredulously): You cannot evaluate a teacher on the performance of his or her students?
> UNION VP: Right.

That was one man's *opinion*, but in New York that opinion became the *law*, because of the power of the teachers union. In 2007, the law allowed New York City Schools Chancellor Joel Klein to consider, among other things, "the extent to which the teacher successfully utilized analysis of available student performance data" when reviewing candidates for tenure, a lifetime appointment.

Of course, that's *not* the same as judging a teacher based on student performance, but the mere possibility of connecting student performance with teacher effectiveness was enough to cause fits at union headquarters. Both the state and city teacher unions lobbied hard for a change, and in April 2008 the legislature went along and changed the law to read, "The teacher shall not be granted or denied tenure based on student performance data."

That's what Richard Iannuzzi, the president of the New York State United Teachers, said in so many words: "Student assessments are designed to assess students, not teachers."

Klein called the legislature's action "unconscionable." Celebrating the victory, then UFT president Randi Weingarten said, "There is no independent or conclusive research that shows you can accurately measure the impact of an individual teacher on a student's academic achievement."

Independent analysts disagree. Eric Hanushek, who specializes in the economics of education at Stanford University, wrote in an email: "It is very clear from the research into variations in teacher quality that such information would be useful. This New York State action says it cannot even be looked at. The implication is that tenure decisions cannot be made on performance."

Calling this "very bad public policy," Professor Hanushek added dryly, "I guess only friendships and politics count – just what the unions have always railed against."

Weingarten denied that her members are afraid of accountability, but this action may put unions into a hole they'll have trouble digging out of, because school administrators have reams of data about student performance, thanks largely to the federal No Child Left Behind law.

Unions are correct to worry about oversimplification. Urged to "drill down" to find out who is learning and who is not, administrators believe they can pinpoint which teachers are effective at teaching certain skills. I've sat with superintendents, principals and department chairs and heard them name teachers who, they said, were either outstanding or deficient at teaching specific skills. "X doesn't seem to be able to teach his students how to multiply with fractions," one educator said, showing me student performance data and contrasting it with data from another teacher's class.

Unfortunately, these administrators did not bring up the make-up of the classes being tested – whether they were new immigrants or students with disabilities or gifted children – even though *who* is being taught clearly affects scores. That's what makes teachers worry, and rightly so.

Test data invites oversimplification because it ignores the fact that students *bring* value (and baggage) to school, just as good teachers *add* value. Unions and administrators have an interest in figuring out how to measure both, if only to ensure that teachers are not penalized for working with difficult-to-teach children.

Because test data is not going to go away, progressive union leadership ought to be lobbying hard for *creative* uses of it, not punitive ones. Forward-looking leadership would be demanding immediate help for teachers, so that they could improve in those areas where the evidence suggests deficiency. It would be helping to create solutions, instead of wielding political power to protect every union member's job. It would be looking for ways to use evidence of student learning in sophisticated ways and in conjunction with other evidence.

Denying that there's any connection between teaching and learning contradicts what experience teaches us, and flies in the face of common sense. If unions are telling us that there's *no* connection between teaching and learning, why support teachers, or public education for that matter?

In August 2010, the *Los Angeles Times* published a story that created a small firestorm in education circles. Three reporters documented the effects that teachers had on their students' test results over a 7-year period. And the *LA Times* named names, so that now the world knew that students in John Smith's 5th grade class start out ahead but lose ground as the year goes on, while Miguel Aguilar's 5th graders follow the opposite trajectory: they do poorly at the start but outscore Mr. Smith's students by year's end.

Those are just two of the names the *LA Times* printed, and the union was furious, calling for a boycott of the paper.

But is it wrong to speak the truth? Is it wrong to call out ineffective teachers? That's the debate, with even the Secretary of Education weighing in on whether it's appropriate to make the names public.

For the record, Secretary Duncan approved. "Too often our systems keep all of our teachers in the dark about the quality of their own work," Duncan told an audience at the Statehouse Convention Center in downtown Little Rock. "In other fields, we talk about success constantly, with statistics and other measures to prove it. Why, in education, are we scared to talk about what success looks like?"

Let's be clear about one thing: the *LA Times* is most definitely NOT breaking new ground when it tells us that some teachers are more effective than others. Every parent knows that, and savvy parents lobby for teacher so-and-so for their children.

One summer evening my wife and I were at a block party where the subject came up. Earlier in the day I was bicycling with friends, and one woman described how hard she had worked to make sure that her twins had a certain math teacher in middle school because, she said, everyone knew she was the best teacher in the school.

I firmly believe that just about everyone in any school can tell you who the really good teachers are in the building. Whether they *will* tell you is another story, perhaps, but everyone knows who's good and who's bad, and I am certain that judgment is based on what students accomplish.

I should qualify that, because 'everyone' does not include union leaders, particularly the NEA's Dennis Van Roekel. He told me that teachers should be judged based on their effort, pure and simple. He called it their 'practice.'

I applaud the *LA Times* for bringing this to the forefront. My qualms about naming names are mitigated by the fact that the *LA Times* had *seven* years of data. That's not a blip subject to the vagaries of testing. However, I worry that releasing scores could be a step backward if it merely heightens the significance of scores on bubble tests, but that's a risk worth taking.

One sentence early in the piece was key, in my view: "Year after year, one 5th-grade class learns far more than the other down the hall."

And then: "In Los Angeles and across the country, education officials have long known of the often huge disparities among teachers. They've seen the indelible effects, for good and ill, on children. But rather than analyze and address these disparities, they have opted mostly to ignore them."

To me, that's the central point: the adults in charge have known of the damage that some teachers are doing—and have done nothing, or nothing effective anyway, about it. That's the high tolerance for mediocrity that I find alarming, and that's what must be addressed, and soon.

Of course it's possible to identify—and help—low performing teachers. In 2008, I watched the chair of the math department in a D.C. high school going over student scores with his faculty. He was able to pinpoint which teachers were apparently not doing a good job of teaching particular concepts (quadratic equations, for example) because he had student results matched up with their teachers. His response was to offer those teachers new strategies and approaches, to give them opportunities to get better. How can anyone find fault with that?

The next step is to remove those teachers who, for whatever reason, do not improve.

So rather than boycott the *LA Times*, I say we should all subscribe. And we should turn up the heat on administrators who refuse to set and maintain high standards for their teachers, and on unions that don't work hard to give teachers opportunities to be excellent.

When I expressed as much on *Taking Note*, hundreds of respondents attacked my reasoning. Knowing that I am an opponent of simple bubble tests and have spoken out on the importance of multiple measures, they wondered how I could get behind a system that was using so-called 'value added' data and nothing else.

I cop to the charge of inconsistency and defend myself thusly: nothing else was happening! It took the press to move the system off the dime, where all the adults have been complacently sitting while students fail to learn.

The approach has major bugs, but, with all its faults, it's a darn sight better than doing nothing about lousy teaching and cowardly administrators.

As one commenter, Peter, wrote: "If the temperature gauge in my car moves toward 'H,' it does not mean necessarily that my engine will seize imminently; maybe my coolant is low or needs replacing. Data is a window we use to help see what's really happening. If my value-added numbers moved in an adverse direction, the next step is to discern why. Is it my instruction? Classroom management? Assessment? If this data's been readily available and teachers need a newspaper article to find it, we have a communication breakdown, which ultimately is a leadership breakdown."

Amen to what Peter has written. To continue his metaphor, the warning light been on in too many engines for too long. In my original post and in subsequent comments, I said that administrators have to be called out as well. And if union contracts stand in the way of helping or removing ineffective teachers, then the union–and the school board–that negotiated the contract ought to be called out as well.

The old system in which the principal visits the classroom a few times a year (often announced in advance) is dying. What will replace it is the question. School administrators might want bubble test scores, or maybe they'd like to be able to rate teachers subjectively. Both of those present real problems, and so I think that the two teacher unions need to move beyond their trade union role and become professional unions, working to help teachers get better and also to remove those who can't cut it.

The IMPACT evaluation system imposed by former D.C. Schools Chancellor Michelle Rhee during her tenure in Washington is controversial, but it's an improvement on a system that ends up giving 95 percent or more of teachers a rating of satisfactory or better, especially when not even 25 percent of students are scoring at a proficient level. In Rhee's system, every teacher is observed five times every year, twice by 'master educators' who work for the central office and three times by administrators in her building. Teachers are rated on a scale of 1-4, and an average of '1' means immediate dismissal, regardless of seniority or tenure. A rating of '2' or lower puts that teacher on notice: she has one year to improve or face dismissal.

One young D.C. teacher who has been through IMPACT said there are advantages to NOT knowing when you are going to be observed: "Every day I had to make sure that my objective was clear, that my kids knew it. Not just the days I got observed. And I think that made my classroom a little bit more consistent, and they learned a little bit more this year than last year."

His endorsement was qualified, however. "My only issue was that it's marketed as a growth tool for teachers, and there weren't as many resources to help that growth as I would have liked to see."

And that's the key issue. Because of the District of Columbia's unique situation, Rhee was able to impose her system; she did not have to negotiate it. Suppose she'd had to negotiate? Is there a union in the nation that would negotiate a system that provided equally for growth and for removal of ineffective teachers?

That's the challenge: defining success. It can't be just test scores, but it has to be real—and failure has to have consequences.

While I do not have unbridled enthusiasm for value added measurement, I am enthusiastic about finally coming to grips with teachers who are persistently ineffective, perhaps because they have stopped caring, perhaps because they didn't belong in the classroom in the first place, perhaps because their administrators played 'sink or swim' with them.

Like the rest of us, teachers want reliable information about restaurants, auto repair shops, hospitals, doctors and so on, but they resist efforts to rate/evaluate their own effectiveness. Is that reasonable?

Some are saying that digital video may transform teacher evaluation, but I am skeptical. Back in March 2010, the NEA's Dennis Van Roekel told me that teachers should be judged based on their 'practice,' but what if *lots* of people are watching that 'practice' and grading it? Would he still be enthusiastic?

Large-scale videotaping experiments are now going on in at least seven districts, including Dallas, Denver, Hillsborough (FL), and Pittsburgh. There about 3000 teachers are allowing themselves to be videotaped, with trained 'graders' viewing their efforts (but not their principals). These graders look for specific behaviors: does a teacher consistently ignore students who have their hands up to answer questions? Does she make an effort to help students who may have missed the previous day's lesson? Does she turn her back on the classroom on a regular basis?

This effort, funded by the Gates Foundation, is being managed by the Educational Testing Service, with the research being conducted by Thomas Kane of Harvard.

What's the endgame? If the goal is to provide tutorial videos that will demonstrate good teaching techniques to struggling teachers, that's one thing. If it's a 'gotcha' game, however, it will be strongly opposed by organized teachers everywhere. As the AFT's Randi Weingarten told the *New York Times* on December 4, 2010, "Videotaped observations have their role but shouldn't be used to substitute for in-person observations to evaluate teachers."

Bill Gates told *New York Times* reporter Sam Dillon that he was interested in helping teachers. "Some teachers are extremely good...What's unbelievable is how little the exemplars have been studied...You have to follow the exemplars."

There's money to be made here. Firms like Teachscape are charging districts hundreds of thousands of dollars to set up systems for schools (one camera per school) so they can video-tape teachers at work. The *NY Times* says Teachscape charges about $1.5 million for a district with 140 schools and 7,000 students for the first year, and $800,000 annually after that.

But let's take a deep breath. This particular project will result in 64,000 hours of classroom video by June 2011, creating what someone has called 'a cottage industry' for retired educators who will now sit and watch and 'grade' what these teachers do.

So far so good, but *how* do those 64,000 hours become short tutorials of the sort that Mr. Gates is envisioning? I work in this business, and for a typical *NewsHour* piece that runs 8 minutes, we will come back from the field with 20-30 hours of video. And we will work for days and days, whittling and shaping so the video tells a story. Who's going to do that with these 64,000 hours?

And because television is little more than 'radio with pictures' and these classroom videos are really nothing more than a wide-angle camera in the back of the room, with a small microphone mounted on top and a mic on the teacher, the sound is going to be awful. Who's going to watch what they cannot hear?

To give you a better idea of just what 64,000 hours means, that's about 2,666 days or 7.3 years of video—all without decent sound. I think I'd rather do hard time in a penitentiary than be sentenced to watch all that.

Or think of it this way. I have been working for PBS since 1985 and in *25 years* have amassed an archive of 90,000 hours of video (professionally recorded with good sound quality). These folks are collecting 64,000 hours in *just the first year alone.*

Lack of evaluation, excessively rigid evaluation and ineffective evaluation – we have three simultaneous serious problems, but what's the solution for our education system? Given that Race to the Top required states to promise to connect the dots between student and teacher performance (just to be eligible to apply), the thoughtful evaluation of teachers matters more than ever. Someone has to decide not only what the criteria are but also *who* does the evaluating – and make sure those evaluators are prepared for the job.

Certainly teachers are being scrutinized more today because of public concern about test scores. Unless it's a violation of the union contract, principals drop in regularly to watch teachers at work. Whether these observations are diagnostic in nature and designed to help teachers improve, an empty ritual that leads to inflated ratings, or a 'gotcha' game is the essential question.

In my experience, most teachers are not afraid of being evaluated. But what do they want? Conversations with teachers over the years suggest that, above all, they want to work in an environment that respects their professionalism and allows and encourages them to improve. The new MetLife survey, discussed above, bears this out. I think of teachers I've watched in Chattanooga, Baltimore and a small town near Seattle; all were expected to plan together and were encouraged to watch each other teach on occasion. Every week they gathered for the school equivalent of a hospital's 'grand rounds,' where they shared insights about students they had in common.

Teachers shouldn't have a problem with student performance scores being part of the evaluation equation, as long as the results allow them to examine and improve their own skills. If Mrs. Smith's students show a good grasp of multiplying fractions and her colleagues' scores do not, then her colleagues would like to know what she's doing. But if those scores are simply used in a 'gotcha' game to reward Mrs. Smith and punish everyone else, expect continuing hostility.

71

6

Paying Teachers

"TEACHERS: Increase Your Salary With A Master's Degree!" the online advertisement screams at its targeted audience. And that advertisement tells you everything you need to know about how we pay teachers (average salary $48,000). It's all about inputs, based on the assumption that the more teachers study, the more their students will learn.

It turns out that's not true. Nor do advanced degrees correlate highly with student achievement. But the way it works now, teachers are paid based on years of experience and number of graduate credits. One estimate puts the Masters degree 'bonus' total at a staggering $8.6 billion. Changing that system is one of public education's biggest challenges. It's a rat's nest, or, as Bill Gates put it in November 2010: "Restructuring pay systems is like kicking a beehive."

Picture the typical salary schedule for teachers. It's probably just a page of small boxes. One axis notes years of service; the other, academic credits beyond the basic Bachelor's degree. As you go up in years and out in credits, you make more money. In the upper right hand corner, in the last box, is the maximum you will earn.

It's like having a crystal ball, because on your very first day on the job you can look well into the future and see just how much (or how little) you will be earning 25, 30 or 35 years from that moment. And it won't matter whether you're the best teacher or the hardest working teacher—or the converse, the worst and laziest. Your salary is set.

My fantasy would be to show that to any successful entrepreneur, say Bill Gates, Oprah Winfrey, John Doerr or Warren Buffett, and get them to share their innermost thoughts about such a system.

Money is now very much in the evaluation conversation, whether it's called "merit pay" or "pay for performance" or something else.

School leaders like Michelle Rhee believe public education needs a system that rewards superior teachers with more money. By superior, she means teachers whose students perform well academically, but that creates problems because not all students in all grades are tested in all subjects.

"Why would you want to change?" asks National Education Association president Dennis Van Roekel. He believes the current system, which he says pays for the skills, knowledge and responsibility of the adults, has evolved over time. "Right now, in fifty states, in over the last fifty years, they've pretty much all kind of moved to the same place," he declared. "Why is that? Why are they using what they use now? Nobody's telling them to. There's no law, or regulation, or requirement. Yet at over fifty years, with over 15,000 school districts, they've moved to the same compensation system. There must be a reason. I believe it's because it works."

Moreover, he says that the current system is much better than previous approaches. "Before that, schools paid teachers based on gender. Men got paid more than women. Relatives of school board got paid more than non-relatives. Elementary teachers got paid less than high school teachers."

He adds another historical note. "In the past, many teachers didn't have a college degree, but they found that, as you got more education, you were better at your skill and you improved with time."

In short, we can expect Van Roekel and the NEA to defend the current system to the fullest because, as he says, "It works."

Pay for performance is a Pandora's box, because if we begin paying more to teachers whose students do well academically, sooner or later the flip side of the issue comes into play: What do we do with teachers whose students aren't learning (again, based on tests)? Should those teachers lose their jobs if reasonable efforts to help them improve don't work?

President Obama weighed in on this issue when he supported a Rhode Island school district's decision to dismiss the faculty and staff at a persistently failing high school. "Our kids get only one chance at an education, and we need to get it right," he told the U.S. Chamber of Commerce in March 2010. And on more than one occasion he has observed, "Too many supporters of my party have resisted the idea of rewarding excellence in teaching with extra pay, even though we know it can make a difference in the classroom."

Performance-based pay is integral to the federal government's Race to the Top strategy, which has awarded multi—million dollar prizes to 11 states and the District of Columbia. Many of the winners made promises about creating pay structures based in part on student learning, but whether they will be able to keep them remains to be seen.

At least one superintendent has decided not to accept the federal dollars because he doesn't believe in merit pay. Bill Mathews, the superintendent of Jones County (GA) schools, is turning down $1.3 million, his share of the state's $400 million award. His stated reason—he doesn't trust the notion of a value-added assessment system for teachers based on standardized test scores. Mathews told the *Atlanta Journal-Constitution* that the research doesn't bear out the effectiveness of these systems, and that implementing one would be too expensive. Educating children is a team effort by all the adults in the building, he said, and to single out teachers in this way was unacceptable. "My philosophy has always been that from the front door to the back door, from the secretary to the lunchroom worker, [everyone] is responsible for the student achievement of every child," Mathews was quoted as saying. "We set our goals and if we meet our goals, we all celebrate."

On the other hand, a handful of districts are experimenting now, including Pittsburgh; Austin and Fort Worth, Texas; Denver; and Baltimore, according to a comprehensive analysis by the Hechinger Institute, the highly regarded education journalism program affiliated with Teachers College, Columbia.

These issues defy black-and-white analysis. If a simple solution existed, we'd probably have come upon it by now. Teacher unions, and quite a few teachers, have consistently rejected the idea of connecting scores and salaries, fearing that administrators will use cheap bubble-test scores to the exclusion of all else.

Then there's the student turnover issue. In cities, it's endemic. When a niece of mine was teaching in Orlando, she told me that half her class typically turned over by mid-January. That's pretty common. And when student turnover reaches 75 to 100 percent in the course of a year, as it does in some urban classrooms, is it possible to know *which* teacher is responsible for *particular* student gains? Who gets the credit: the teacher at the beginning of the year, the one who taught most of the material mid-year or the teacher who administered the test at year's-end?

Complications aside, the tide seems to be moving inexorably toward connecting the dots between teacher pay and student performance. What we don't know yet is what form this will take.

This 'faddishness' would be rejected if people knew their history, Richard Rothstein suggests. The highly respected research associate of the Economic Policy Institute and former *New York Times* education columnist says, "There has never been any research that shows this works, although it's fashionable to think that it should work." Rothstein fears that, since only math and reading lend themselves to easy testing, the curriculum will be further narrowed, an eventuality he believes would be "disastrous." He went on to explain what he believes will happen: "The best way to get higher test scores is to prep for tests, to give a lot of instruction in test preparation and test-taking skills, not in the underlying subject. It's to focus on the children who are closest to the passing point and ignore other children. There are all kinds of ways that we can boost test scores that don't contribute to improved instruction."

Will putting money on the table make teachers better? Will teachers become more effective if a significant bonus is dangled before them? Opponents of merit pay got a boost in September 2010 when the National Center on Performance Incentives at Vanderbilt University released the results of a 3-year controlled study in which 143 middle school teachers in Nashville were offered as much as $15,000 in bonuses if they could increase their students' math scores. These teachers were matched with comparable teachers, who were given $100 for participating.

Matt Springer, who led the study, told the *NewsHour* how it turned out. "The conclusion of the report is that opportunities to earn a large financial incentive didn't increase student performance. It didn't change teacher behavior overwhelmingly."

In other words, those who could earn a bonus and those who could not delivered the same results. Money made no difference.

Added Springer, "That's not to say that compensation reform and pay-for performance can't have a meaningful impact.

It just means that we can't just put money out there and expect that it's going to change our education system. Pay is never going to be the magic bullet."

In fact, some teachers were offended by the study's premise. "Do they think we aren't giving 100 percent now?" one indignant teacher asked.

The study's findings notwithstanding, 11 of the 12 winners of Race to the Top grants have agreed to develop plans for performance-based pay. Whether there will be actual dollars on the table remains to be seen.

The NEA's Van Roekel also opposes merit pay because, as he says, it's expensive. "Do the math," he challenges. "If there's a set pot of money and the best teachers make a lot more, then others have to have their pay cut, unless the public is willing to pay more. "It will cost more money. I guarantee it will cost more money. And so if your plan doesn't build in a sustainable revenue source to manage that program, it won't work."

Setting aside money for merit pay is not the approach taken by many economists- nor by Bill Gates. These experts are attacking the current system, which they believe to be irrational. It makes no sense whatsoever to pay teachers based on seniority and graduate credits, they say, because there's scant evidence that either actually benefits students. In his speech to the Council of the Chief State School Officers, Gates said, "My own state of Washington has an average salary bump of nearly $11,000 for a master's degree – and more than half of our teachers get it. That's more than $300 million every year that doesn't help kids," he said.

"And that's one state," he added. Nearly half of all teachers in the United States have Masters degrees, bringing them salary bumps of up to $10,000 per year. Most of these advanced degrees in are in education, not specific subject matter.

How the current system of paying teachers is going to

change is the question, not *whether*. Given the political strength of teacher unions, it's likely that the changes will affect only the newly hired, but things are going to be different. Stay tuned.

7

Keeping Teachers

On a warm spring afternoon in Texas, about 25 education majors, all young white women, are waving plastic toys in the air, giggling and singing "Row, Row, Row Your Boat." They're pretending to be 5-year-olds as part of their teacher training.

In rural Georgia, 1,200 miles to the east, a young man is leading his ninth-grade English class through the day's vocabulary. One of the words is 'strenuous,' which he has written on the board as 'strenous.' During the lesson he reviews the definition, the spelling and the syllabification, never catching his mistake. His students dutifully copy his spelling mistake into their workbooks.

And in Oakland, California, an 11th grade biology class is having its 167th consecutive class without a certified science teacher; they've had a parade of substitute teachers for an entire year.

Taken together, these anecdotes would seem to indicate that we are facing a major crisis in teaching – that we need more teachers and we need better-trained teachers.

However, the plural of anecdote is not data, and so I would make a different argument. I believe these vignettes, and the circumstances behind them, demonstrate that our education system has an unacceptably high tolerance for mediocrity, and that national, state and local policies merely reinforce the status quo.

Some regions of the country will always have a difficult time recruiting teachers, and many districts have trouble finding and keeping science, math and special education teachers, but we actually produce more teachers than we need. Where persistent shortages exist, these are generally self-inflicted wounds which fall into three categories: Schools underpay and mistreat teachers and eventually drive them from the profession; inept school districts cannot find the qualified teachers living under their noses; and substandard training ill-prepares young men and women for the realities of classroom life.

Imagine a swimming pool with a serious leak. You wouldn't expect that pouring more and more water into the pool would, in time, fix the leak – but that's precisely the approach we are taking toward the so-called teacher shortage. Everyone's noticed that the teaching 'pool' is low, and getting lower. The response has been to recruit more people into teaching, using a variety of strategies including PSA campaigns, millions of federal dollars, hiring bonuses, help with mortgages and recruitment trips to Spain and other distant lands.

(Most of this is not new. Almost every U.S. President since Harry Truman has warned of teacher shortages, and large-scale recruitment efforts have followed. These days President Obama and Secretary Duncan are warning of an imminent shortage of teachers. The more things change...)

Yet the pool keeps losing water because no one is paying attention to the leak. That is, we're misdiagnosing the problem as "recruitment" when it's really "retention." Simply put, we train teachers poorly and then treat them badly – and so they leave in droves. (Just how many leave is not clear, although everyone repeats the same statistic: 50 percent leave within their first five years. That seems to come from a 2003 study by Richard Ingersoll and others, which asserts that 50 percent leave their *first* as-signment within five years—but don't necessarily leave the profession. And while there's a huge difference between changing schools and changing professions, whenever a teacher leaves a school, it has to recruit and hire a replacement. In 2009 Ingersoll and colleagues put the 5-year number at 40 percent.)

Whether the actual number is 30, 40 or 50 percent, the issue is not trivial. In a November 2010 report, the well-respected National Commission on Teaching and America's Future put the cost of what ought to be called a "teacher dropout problem" at more than $7 billion a year. It's expensive to recruit and then 'in-duct' rookies, year after year, even when induction is the minimal 'sink or swim' approach.

As it happens, new evidence indicates increased interest in teaching among our nation's university students. Survey after survey of entering college freshmen reveals that more than 10 per-cent say they want to teach after graduation. Perhaps because of a failing economy, the recent results are the best showing for the teaching profession since the early 1970s and almost twice what they were in 1982, the lowest point of interest in teaching.

On the surface, this news is encouraging. But just be-cause more undergraduates want to teach, and just because Teach For America is flooded with applications, no one should assume we're out of the woods. We aren't.

The fact remains that our nation's schools and colleges of education already produce more than enough teachers. But about 30 percent of newly minted teachers don't go into classrooms. Some never intended to; they majored in education because it's an easy way to get a degree or so they could have a "fall back" option. Others found they couldn't get teaching jobs in their hometown, so they found other work; in other words, *staying home* was the goal, not being a teacher. Those who avoid teaching may be making a wise career move, because teaching is often hard and unrewarding work, particularly for rookies, and particularly in cities.

While shortages exist in some regions of the country and in some subjects, the harsh truth is that our persistent teacher shortage is a self-inflicted wound.

The real problems lie within the system that is already in place, and no influx of idealistic men and women will change that. In my reporting for PBS in 1999, I found that school administrators in Georgia frequently assigned teachers to teach subjects regardless of whether they had majored, or even minored, in those subjects in college. For example, the young man who couldn't spell 'strenuous' was actually a junior high school physical education teacher and coach, but he'd been assigned to teach English, history and math at the local high school instead. He knew he was in over his head, but he had no choice. In that particular high school, at least 20 percent of faculty members were teaching classes in subjects they hadn't themselves studied.

In other places we found qualified, certified teachers who simply couldn't penetrate incompetent school bureaucracies. For two consecutive years Katherine Scheuermann, who earned a California license to teach science, applied for a teaching position in Oakland. She finally got a response in year three--a letter inviting her to apply for a position in bilingual education. Without much difficulty we found two other certified teachers who told essentially the same story: Oakland's bureaucracy was impenetrable, so they looked elsewhere.

Those who do get hired to teach in cities aren't likely to stay long. American cities lose teachers at an alarming rate. For example, for years Oakland has been losing up to 30 percent of its teachers every year, even though it pays well for a school district. Why do science teachers leave? Ask veteran Nancy Caruso:

I had no water, and I was supposed to teach science. I was toting water from a decaying toilet, basically little gallon containers, one at a time, and it was just very frustrating for me. And if you look around, I'm in a decaying building. It's graffiti ridden, trash everywhere, and it seems like nothing that could get done gets done.

New teachers seemed to be treated even worse. As Caruso, who left after 10 years at Oakland High School, wryly observed:

Administrators give new teachers the hardest, most challenging classes and the most preparations, so they have maybe four different classes to prepare for every day, and then administrators expect that that's going to make them excited about teaching. It's just not conducive to retaining young, enthusiastic people. They get burnt out and so they go to the suburbs or they leave teaching completely.

But the roots of mediocrity and incompetence can be found at many of the institutions that train teachers. They tend to treat their education programs more as "cash cows" for their overall needs, diverting tuition paid by education majors into law, medicine, engineering and nursing programs. As Linda Darling-Hammond of Stanford University notes, "If you are preparing to be a teacher, you can expect about half of the tuition money you put into the till to come back to support your preparation."

Training teachers on the cheap means large classes on campus, rather than intensive (and more expensive) work in real schools with real children. So, for example, we found those would-be teachers at Texas A&M earnestly pretending to be 5-year-olds for 50 minutes at a stretch. "It's as close as we can get to the real thing," one student told us, apparently unaware of the existence of a dozen elementary schools within a few miles of campus.

Training on the cheap means more part-time faculty and lower salaries for those with full-time jobs. It's no secret that schools of education are at the bottom of the university pecking order and those who actually train teachers are on the very bottom of the pile, the lowest rung of the ladder.

It's likely that unimaginative training has an unintended consequence: breeding contempt for the profession these students are supposed to be getting ready for. We asked a class of seniors, on the verge of graduating and moving into classrooms, whether they were having doubts about their career choice. Virtually every hand went up.

At least some of the faculty at Texas A&M and every other school of education actually know how to train teachers well, but that requires more time and money. That year about 30 percent of A&M's education students were enrolled in a separate and much more demanding program that required them to spend 40 hours a week working with a mentor teacher in a public school. Throughout the year, these students took most of their university classes in the public school, often taught by experienced public school teachers.

Where were the university's education professors? Most were back on campus, lecturing, writing and doing research, and for good reason: They won't get tenure for doing a good job of training teachers, but they might if they do enough research and publish enough articles.

Competition from alternative certification programs is forcing education schools to shape up, as noted in a previous chapter. These alternate programs, which have been designed to attract and train older professionals looking to change careers, generally provide an intensive summer of training and a year of weekend meetings, a far cry from the four- or five-year ed school programs. Some alternative certification programs are suspect, but others seem to be effective. For example, graduates of a state-run alternative program in Austin that same year were routinely outperforming graduates of nearly every education school in Texas on the state test for teachers.

Recruiting teachers is an appealingly simple solution to a complex problem. It's also the wrong approach. It not only lets education schools off the hook; it actually rewards them. After all, those federal training dollars are going to be spent at schools of education. It also treats them as part of the solution, which in one way is akin to asking the polluters to clean up the river. On the other hand, alternative programs are unlikely to produce enough teachers to fill the system's needs, and so schools of education have to be 'transformed,' as that November 2010 NCATE report urges.

Public school systems, with their 'sink or swim' approach to new teachers, are a huge part of the problem. What other organization takes such a cavalier attitude toward human capital? Most organizations invest serious resources in the recruitment and training of employees, the goal being to see them succeed. Why go out and spend those dollars again, year after year? But public education doesn't seem to care, at least not enough to change its ways.

Current national policy toward recruiting and retaining teachers seems to be a waste of money, as well as a strategy that's destined to fail. As Richard Ingersoll of the University of Pennsylvania told us, "we can recruit all kinds of qualified people and persuade them to go into teaching, but if they get into jobs that aren't well paid and don't have particularly good working conditions in which they're given little say in the way schools operate, it's not going to really solve the problem because a lot of these people will leave."

Professor Ingersoll is correct. *If* teacher training were challenging, and *if* teaching were a well-paid occupation – in which expertise was respected and teachers were given opportunities to collaborate and improve – and *if* out-of-field teaching were

85

simply unacceptable, there would be no teacher shortage. Attending to those conditions would fix the leak.

As I have written elsewhere in these pages, technology has turned the world upside down. Schools can no longer be places where children are just expected to answer questions. Instead, teachers must encourage questions, and more questions. They must help youth sort through the flood of information that surrounds them daily.

I hope schools of education are up to the challenge of training a new breed of teachers. I have my doubts, but let's give them a chance. I hope school systems are prepared to drop 'sink or swim' as a way of working with human capital, but there too I have my doubts.

8

Who Needs Tenure?
Why Senority?

"If I could change one thing, I would get rid of tenure." – Larry Rosenstock, founder of High Tech High and winner of the 2010 McGraw Prize in Education, at a public forum, September 2010

"So would I." – Stephen McMahon, President of San Jose (CA) Teachers Union, in response.

"I could care less about tenure." – Dal Lawrence, former president of the Toledo Federation of Teachers, in an interview, November 2010

"I have started using the words 'due process' myself. I think 'tenure' is a loaded word." – Randi Weingarten, President of the American Federation of Teachers, in an email, November 2010

What on earth is going on here? Is the question of tenure actually up for debate and discussion? If so, it's long overdue. And is it possible that teacher unions will take the initiative?

Teacher tenure is closely connected to the flawed evaluation process. After all, an evaluation system that finds 97 percent of teachers to be satisfactory or better will have no trouble handing out lifetime jobs.

"Tenure should be a significant and consequential milestone in a teacher's career," notes the National Council on Teacher Quality. "Unfortunately, the awarding of tenure occurs virtually automatically in just about all states, with little deliberation or consideration of evidence of teacher performance. Teacher effectiveness in the classroom, rather than years of experience, should be the preponderant criterion in tenure decisions."

In the current system, most public school teachers gain tenure, generally speaking a lifetime job, after just three years of teaching. In eight states, including California and Maryland, tenure is granted after two years. Hawaii and Mississippi offer tenure after just one year, and our nation's capital requires no set amount of teaching performance before granting tenure. In other words, many school administrators are forced to make this critical and lasting decision halfway through a teacher's first or second year in the classroom.

That stands in sharp contrast to the tenure process in higher education. There it's far harder to achieve, the process taking as long as seven years in 4-year institutions and three years in community colleges. Today not even one-third of those teaching in college have tenure, a percentage that is dropping as colleges increasingly turn to part-time instructors.

More than half of those hired to teach in colleges and universities are not placed on the tenure track. That is, they have *no* hope of achieving a lifetime appointment.

Tenure on campus is said to protect academic freedom. Professors are free to challenge conventional wisdom without fear of being summarily fired, for example. They can resist pressure from administrators to give out high grades, for example. And tenure is said to encourage thinking and challenges to the conventional wisdom. Tenure evolved out of excesses, professors being fired because of pressure from wealthy donors or politicians, for example. And tenure is disappearing because of financial pressures.

In my conversations about public education, tenure is always *the* hot button issue, which may explain the statements from union leaders that lead this chapter. Perhaps they are trying to defuse the volatility. Good luck with that, because the heart of the matter is not tenure itself but the difficulty of removing incompetent teachers, men and women who should never have been granted tenure in the first place.

That's the adjective I hear most often – 'incompetent.' But incompetence in the classroom is rarely the reason a teacher is fired. The grounds for termination are more likely to be taken from this list: immorality, persistent violation of school rules, unprofessional conduct, commission of a felony or sexual harassment. Unsatisfactory performance and the catchall "evident unfitness to teach" are harder to prove, apparently.

Everyone—including many teachers I have met – has stories of simply horrendous teachers who remain on the job. It's the 'why' of the story that gets complicated. Union leaders say they are simply doing their job, protecting a member's due process rights, when they defend a teacher accused of incompetence or egregious behavior. "The real issue is whether teachers should have due process protections, as many of us have been trying to ensure that tenure is simply that," AFT President Randi Weingarten wrote in an email in November 2010. "We don't condone the excesses, nor the fact that management has not done its job to assess teachers effectively or fairly," she added.

Union people tend to blame administrators for not following the rules, but often the rules are Byzantine in their complexity. And those rules were hammered out in bargaining sessions and put in a contract, which was then signed by both parties.

Administrators I have known simply throw up their hands and participate in "the dance of the lemons" or "passing the trash." They somehow find a way to transfer that teacher to another school or another district. (When I was teaching in public high school, one particularly inept English teacher was 'promoted' to be in charge of audio-visual, but that safety valve may not be available in these tough times.)

And on to seniority. Seniority privileges are important in systems that devalue teachers and discourage challenges and experimentation. That probably describes most school systems, which is why teachers value the privileges of seniority: They cannot be moved around on management whim. Reform requires dramatic changes in how teachers are valued; when that happens, seniority won't be an issue. But the first step must, I believe, be taken by teachers and their unions.

Where seniority rules, new teachers suffer. They are often assigned to the least desirable schools, given the worst classes, the most preparations and the additional assignments nobody else wants. But here's a radical thought: Seniority, at least in its most rigid forms, can hurt *veteran* teachers, too.

It's not difficult to find administrators who dislike the rigidities of seniority. When I asked an assistant principal how his elementary school went about hiring teachers, he answered wryly: "You want to know how we fill vacancies? *We* don't. A day or two before school opens, someone shows up with some paperwork and says, 'I'm your new fourth-grade teacher. Where's my classroom?' And we take the paperwork and point to the empty room."

His distaste was palpable. "What other profession doesn't allow the professionals to select their colleagues?" he wanted to know. "How can we create a genuine learning environment when we can't control who teaches here?"

When teachers have seniority, who benefits? That's a question I've been pondering ever since I happened to meet Marlene, a middle-aged veteran of more than 20 years in the classroom.

"This is the worst school I've ever taught in," the teacher muttered to herself, just loud enough for me to hear. We were watching several hundred high school students streaming into school on a fall morning. I asked how long she'd been teaching there. "It's my first year," she said bitterly.

Because her union was fiercely protective of teachers' seniority rights, I assumed she'd made the decision to teach there, and I asked her why. Her answer stunned me: "It's the closest school to my home, and I wanted a short commute."

We introduced ourselves and talked for a while. I don't know what sort of teacher Marlene is, but it's easy to hypothesize that she's a burned-out, bored worker counting the hours until she can go home for the day. I can imagine her contempt for the school playing itself out with her students.

Is Marlene "Exhibit A," proving the evils of the seniority system, or could there be more to the story? I'm assuming that 20 or 25 years ago she was a typical new teacher: idealistic, energetic and determined to contribute to the growth and learning of her students. What happened to make her view her profession through such a narrow prism? Had the rewards of teaching been so slight that *commuting time*, rather than her colleagues, the curriculum or the work environment, was her highest priority?

In my understanding of history, education's seniority system emerged in part because of the high-handed treatment teachers received at the hands of administrators. That is, unions fought for seniority to protect their members from the arbitrary decisions of administrators, and any veteran teacher can tell horror stories of being treated contemptuously or indifferently. Does that still happen? Do administrators still treat trained teachers as if they were interchangeable parts? Sadly, in many places they do.

A few years ago I watched a first-year teacher showing high school sophomores how to determine the area of a rectangle. She gave her students the formula and did three sample problems on the board. Each time she gave the answer in meters. No one in the class, including the teacher, knew that the answers had to be in *square* meters.

What she was experiencing in her first year on the job helps explain why unions fight so hard for teachers' rights. As a new teacher, she had no rights at all, and she was treated disrespectfully. The school district had hired her to teach *physical education*, the subject she'd trained to teach, but on the first day of school her principal assigned her to teach two sections of algebra, a subject she herself had not studied since high school. Could she have refused? "Yes," she said, smiling ruefully, "but I wouldn't have had a job."

Teachers as Interchangeable Parts seemed to be this school's operating principle. Elsewhere in the school, an art teacher was teaching basic math and a middle school basketball coach was teaching high school English.

That fundamental attitude of anti-professionalism goes beyond individual administrators. It's built into laws and regulations. For example, Georgia (where that young woman was teaching) said at the time that it was fine for teachers to spend up to 40 percent of their time teaching subjects out of their field without being categorized as "out-of-field."

A persuasive analogy, perhaps, can be made with automobiles. Consider this: A BMW mechanic could not spend 40 percent of his time repairing Volvos or Fords, but a phys ed teacher can be told to teach two physics classes! So cars are more important than children (or other people's children, anyway).

The world of teachers is one of small victories, and dozens of routine indignities: constant interruptions from the main office ("Please send Joey Brown to the office"), hall patrol, lunch room duty and the impossibility of taking a bathroom break when nature calls.

Over the years this treatment takes its toll. Many teachers simply leave. As noted earlier, the data show that over 40 percent of new teachers quit the profession in the first five years, according to Richard Ingersoll, professor of education and sociology at the University of Pennsylvania; that's an exit rate far higher than in law, medicine, nursing or the ministry – professions that teaching is often compared to. In many districts, the numbers are even worse. The University of Chicago's Urban Education Institute reported in June 2009 that in Chicago: "Teacher mobility rates at schools with low teacher commitment are abysmal – 67 percent in elementary schools leave within five years, and 76 percent turn over in the high schools. These are schools where teachers do not feel loyal to their schools, would not recommend their school to parents, and do not look forward to teaching every day."

What happens to those who stay? While thousands continue to do wonderful work, despite it all many become, in the current lingo, "burned out." That is, they're on the job, but they've lost sight of why they became teachers in the first place. Perhaps that's what happened to Marlene.

Seniority gives veterans – finally – the opportunity to thumb their noses at these indignities, and that's how I explain Marlene's way of choosing her school.

There are alternatives, ways to allow teachers to be professionals. In Seattle, for instance, progressive union leadership and a visionary superintendent, the late John Stanford, pushed through an agreement allowing teachers to be part of the hiring process at individual schools, while at the same time allowing schools to hire without regard to seniority. That meant teachers were able, for the first time in their professional lives, to participate in choosing their colleagues, in building a professional team at their workplace.

Improving the system, however, cannot *start* with doing away with seniority. Most teachers I've known want to be good at their jobs, but they're working in systems that don't let that happen. Seniority is a desperate protection, but if I were a teacher I'd fight to hold onto it, until management demonstrated its commitment to teaching as a profession.

Teacher unions are necessary, but it seems to me that some unions have for many years done more harm than good for the clientele of the public schools, our children. Ask 'who benefits?' and the answer is obvious: Teachers and their union leaders seem to end up tied for first, while kids come in third. (And in a few cases, the union leaders have put their interests ahead of those of teachers!)

The responsibility (blame) for the mess we are in is shared equally by weak school boards that caved in to union demands, and protectionist and regressive teacher unions. And while it's tempting to say "a plague on both their houses," we don't have that luxury, because both must be part of any solution.

My personal sympathies are with those administrators who want better teachers but are hamstrung by complex rules, and with those teachers who are disgusted by colleagues whose work habits bring dishonor to the profession.

One reason charter schools continue to gain momentum is the opportunity they afford to start over on management/labor relations, unencumbered by complex existing contracts with teacher unions. This doesn't mean that charter schools and unions cannot co-exist, as Steve Barr and his Green Dot charter schools demonstrated when he signed a contract with the American Federation of Teachers. But it's a blank slate, a chance to work out an agreement that gives some weight to the interests of children, who, after all, do not have a union.

Section Two:

Follow the Leader

9

Leadership's Revolving Door

When I began writing this chapter, nine large city school districts were looking for superintendents, including Tucson, St. Louis, Houston and Pittsburgh. Other smaller cities like East Baton Rouge, LA, were also in the market for new superintendents. And whenever you happen to be reading this, it's a safe bet that many cities are searching for leadership.

My old hometown, the District of Columbia, has often been in the hunt, having gone through four superintendents in eight years and two acting chiefs in eight months. During that quest, the District suffered the public humiliation of being turned down by two well-respected educators: Rudy Crew and Carl Cohn. Then in 2007, Washington broke the mold (in both senses of the word) by hiring a young woman who had never even been a school principal, let alone a superintendent. Michelle Rhee, backed by a strong mayor, began turning the Washington schools on their ear from day one on the job.

However, most large districts, including pre-Rhee D.C., approach the process in pretty much the same way. They hire a search firm that specializes in education and pay it many thousands of dollars. The winning search firm goes out and interviews potential candidates, usually men who have left, or want to leave, other superintendencies. At some point, the search firm presents two, three, maybe four "finalists" (again, usually men), who supposedly represent the cream of the crop to the board of education, which makes the final decision. And it's usually some guy who's been around the track a few times.

At the risk of sounding unkind, I find this a bit like shopping at the recycling center – a bizarre game of musical chairs. As with teacher seniority, it's fair to ask, 'who benefits?' from this ritual.

Another flaw in the search approach limits chances for success. School districts hire just one person, not a team, and when that individual arrives, he has to spend a lot of time and energy figuring out which of his inherited colleagues are trustworthy and competent, who resents regime change and who welcomes it. That minefield has destroyed many a capable leader.

Typically, a new superintendent arrives in a city and is hailed as the answer to every problem: low scores, poor attendance, and embarrassing graduation rates. He creates some new (or new-sounding) programs. When change does not occur overnight, disappointment sets in. The superintendent departs for a new city, and the cycle begins anew.

Instead of producing candidates with the hard-eyed management skills and single-minded concentration needed to figure out how best to teach kids, the search process gives these school systems more of the same.

What's striking, at least to this observer, is how unimaginative and predictable this process is. Just as the National Football League, the National Basketball Association and Major League Baseball seem to play musical chairs with their coaches/managers, search firms recycle superintendents. No matter how long and hard these companies search, they inevitably seem to turn up the usual suspects: career educators, most of them white men.

In the fall of 2004, for example, only 16 of the superintendents in the 63 largest districts were women. Five years later, in the 2009-2010 school year, the needle had barely moved:

Women were leading just 18 of the nation's 66 largest big-city school districts. According to Michael Casserly, executive director of the Council of the Great City Schools, "This percentage is actually way above national averages. While women are still a minority among urban superintendents, they are even more underrepresented in the suburbs, small towns and rural areas."

Nationally, the numbers have gotten better, according to "The American School Superintendent: 2010 Dicennial Study," released late in 2010. It reports that the percentage of female superintendents has increased substantially since 1992. In this study of 2000 superintendents, nearly one in four respondents (24.1 percent) was a woman; ten years earlier, the percentage was only 13.2.

In addition to virtually ignoring the talent pool of women, the superintendent search process is faddish to a fault. For several years retired military leaders were all the rage, inspired by the remarkable success of Major General John Stanford in Seattle. That approach was not a panacea, as Washington discovered when it hired its own general. Nobody seemed to realize that it was what General Stanford *did* in Seattle that improved the schools, not where he had worked earlier. After that, districts turned to attorneys: Joel Klein in New York City, Alan Bersin in San Diego and earlier, David Hornbeck in Philadelphia. (Hornbeck lasted six years, Bersin five, before being shown the door. Klein resigned at the end of 2010, after eight generally successful years.)

As it happens, one of the men who turned Washington down, Carl Cohn, described in detail what needs to be done. Cohn, former superintendent in Long Beach, Calif., told the *Washington Post*: "It has to be made clear to everyone that this is about the kids. Then you bring in a take-no-prisoners company that addresses the fundamental issues of operation, of people not doing their jobs."

In that interview, Cohn specifically referenced St. Louis, an urban district that matches Washington, D.C., when it comes to underperformance. For example, 23 percent of K-5 students, 13 percent of middle school students and only 5 percent of St. Louis high school juniors tested at or above the "proficient" level in reading in 2002, despite the district's spending more than $11,000 per pupil.

In 2003, St. Louis took the bold step of hiring a bankruptcy firm to run the schools for a year. The New York firm, Alvarez & Marsal, prefers to call its work "restructuring and turnaround," but rescuing bankrupt companies is its goal, and its method is best described as "take-no-prisoners." Alvarez & Marsal sent Bill Roberti (now a managing director) and a team that had worked together on other projects to St. Louis. Roberti took charge early in June 2003 with a mandate to make the system financially and operationally efficient. Sensibly, "education reform" was not his mandate because Roberti, a businessman who once ran Brooks Brothers, had never worked in education.

The day after Roberti took charge, he and the school board learned from the departing superintendent that the projected budget surplus of $37 million was actually a deficit of at least $35 million and perhaps as much as $90 million.

Roberti and his team went to work. They closed 16 schools and sold 40 properties. They outsourced some school services, including transportation, food services and custodial care. In his year in St. Louis, Roberti gave pink slips to more than 1,400 employees – without laying off a single teacher. When school opened in fall 2004, St. Louis had 5,000 employees, not 7,000, although many of those laid off were then hired by the private bus, food and janitorial vendors. Roberti was harshly criticized by elements in the community but remained unrepentant. "This is not a jobs program," said Roberti, nearly jumping out of his chair to make the point. "This is a school system that is supposed to teach kids, not to provide jobs to the community. It is a business enterprise. Its outcome is student achievement, not providing jobs to the community."

He added, "I think that the public has a right to the same level of expertise in management, whether it's a school business or any kind of business that's public and trades stock. People should be held accountable."

"Financially, the school system was flying blind," Vincent Schoemehl, a school board member at the time and former mayor of St. Louis, told *Education Week*. "The transparency is infinitely improved. We know to the nickel where we are. We've demonstrated that there is a way to connect the cultures of the private sector with the culture of urban education. I would recommend the model to any public entity that needs to refresh itself."

I asked Roberti whether educators could be trusted to fix their own systems. "No, I don't think so," he replied without hesitation. "Educators are an absolutely important component here but only one piece of the equation. St. Louis schools are a $500 million enterprise. Miami's a $4.2 billion enterprise. New York is probably $11 billion. These are big enterprises with lots of complex issues and problems, not just a bunch of classrooms with kids."

Roberti was not hired to fix the city's education problems, but he did not ignore them. He asked the Council of the Great City Schools to come in to assess the system, an act that CGCS's Casserly said was "a bit like the battalion commander calling in an air strike on his own position."

Casserly and his team did not mince words. "St. Louis' instructional program was among the worst that we had seen in any major city across the country," they reported. "The school district has no instructional focus; it lacks a plan for raising student achievement; its instructional staff is poorly organized; and its sense of direction has splintered. The district is also marked by little sense of urgency for improving achievement, no accountability for results, and very low expectations for children.

"To make matters worse," the private report continued, "the district has piled one program on top of another for so many years that one cannot tell what the system is trying to do academically and why."

The report also noted that middle management demonstrated a strong reluctance to change what it was doing, as well as an exceptionally high tolerance for mediocrity. During the year, school attendance improved, but Casserly and Roberti agreed that it would take several years to see significant academic improvement.

William Tate, education department chair at Washington University in St. Louis, criticized Alvarez & Marsal for failing to build public support for the drastic cuts and for ignoring academics. "If you're running a restaurant, you need to have your accounting in order, but you don't stop serving food," Mr. Tate told *Education Week*. "It's important to have your financial place in order, but it's mandatory, when as an organization your mission is teaching and learning, to pay attention to education. They don't talk about academics."

Although Roberti did not claim that he and his team solved all of St. Louis' financial and operational problems, he has no patience with those who wish he'd never been hired. "Some people still believe that they don't have a problem. Those people are saying, 'Give us our system back.' Well, where do you want to go back to? The 23, the 13, and the 5 percent of kids reading at a proficient level? Is that what you want back?"

Fortunately, there is help for urban districts. The Eli & Edythe Broad Foundation has established a training academy to prepare business leaders and other talented individuals from outside the world of education to run urban districts.

Other cities might want to heed Roberti's recipe for fixing urban education. "It's a little bit like alcoholism," he said. "First, you've got to admit you have a problem, and then you have to move to solve it. And you cannot fix the education problems until the operating and financial systems are in order." That, then, is the question cities must ask about their public schools: Is the system broken? Is it educationally bankrupt? As the lawyers say, "Asked and answered."

St. Louis paid Alvarez & Marsal just over $4.4 million for its one year of work, during which time Roberti claimed that he and his team "took $65 million worth of cost out of the system." The $90 million budget deficit was reported to be down to about $20 million when Roberti left, but after his departure it almost immediately ballooned to $38 million.

Did Alvarez & Marsal leave St. Louis schools better off than it found them? That seems to depend on whom you ask. "The general morale in the St. Louis public schools is lower than I have ever seen it," the Rev. B.T. Rice, a member of a local civic group called the St. Louis Black Leadership Roundtable, told *Education Week*. School board meetings were marked by yelling and other disruptions, including chair throwing. On the other hand, Robbyn Wahby, an education aide to the mayor at the time, said she believed the district to be steadily moving in the right direction and praised the management firm for building a strong foundation.

As for Alvarez & Marsal, it moved on to New Orleans, where it signed two multi-million dollar contracts to bring order to the school district there. What precipitated this contract was the discovery that roughly $70 million in federal funds could not be properly accounted for. That led state education officials to compel the Orleans Parish School Board to hire Alvarez & Marsal.

I caught up with Roberti and his colleagues in New Orleans a few weeks after Hurricane Katrina and the subsequent flooding that devastated the city – and destroyed many of the school system's financial records. Katrina kept some school staff out of prison, Roberti told me one afternoon, because a lot of people had been stealing the system blind. He said one employee had been on paid administrative leave for more than a dozen years!

Alvarez & Marsal also received mixed reviews for its work in New Orleans. Its most strident critic may be the man who became superintendent after Alvarez & Marsal's contract expired and the state created the Recovery School District after the hurricane.

"That was a waste of money," said Paul Vallas, the veteran leader from Chicago and Philadelphia. "I'd love to have those millions now, to pay for instructional programs."

Hiring a bankruptcy firm is obviously not a magic bullet. In fact, it's more an act of desperation. And it will fail if the school board and the mayor continue their micromanaging. It will fail if the mayor and the board continue to treat the school system as a jobs program for adults. But even with the odds stacked high against it, a bankruptcy firm could be a viable option, if only because it has the freedom to do what others cannot: take drastic steps and then ride out of town. Roberti and the St. Louis school board knew that going in. As Roberti told me, "The board brought a firm in from outside to do this difficult work because they believed no one inside the city limits could do this and live here when it was over. No one inside the city of St. Louis could get away with doing some of the things that had to be done and live here later without suffering the consequences of it."

That sounds a lot better than a never-ending game of musical chairs.

10

Following Leaders

Michelle Rhee

"I'm going to fire somebody in a little while," the young superintendent said. "Do you want to see that?"

In our world, "see" means "videotape." Washington, D.C., Schools Chancellor Michelle Rhee was actually inviting us to film her as she fired one of her employees.

My colleagues Jane Renaud and Cat McGrath had spent the morning in Chancellor Rhee's office, filming her meeting with parents, community groups and principals. A dynamo, Rhee moved easily from meeting to meeting, seemingly unaware of the presence of our camera.

Jane and Cat were stunned by her invitation, but not so much that they didn't accept on the spot. As Jane recalls, "She told us to come back at a specific time, and so we got a sandwich, returned to her office, set up the equipment and shot the meeting."

That event, shown on national television on the *NewsHour*, helped create the media persona of Michelle Rhee: the fearless and determined reformer who puts the interests of children first.

How we ended up in her office in the first place is a somewhat complicated tale.

Rhee was unknown to those outside the world of education reform when Washington's newly elected mayor, Adrian Fenty, asked her to become chancellor of the public schools that he had just taken control of and had promised to turn into a world-class system. No small challenge, since D.C.'s students scored at the very bottom of the pile on the National Assessment of Educational Progress.

When I read about the appointment of a 37-year-old Korean-American who had never even been a school principal, let alone a superintendent, I talked with my colleagues about chronicling her efforts on the *NewsHour*. All agreed that it could be history in the making and she sounded like an appealing character for television. I was determined to call her, introduce myself and make the pitch.

However, another strong leader – this one a proven commodity – had just accepted the challenge of leading another dreadful school system. That story also intrigued us.

Paul Vallas

I met Paul Vallas in 1996 when he was CEO of the Chicago Public Schools, which had just recently been put under the mayor's control. Not an educator by training, Vallas stepped down from his post as Mayor Daley's budget director to accept the challenge. Tall and gangly, Vallas, then 43 years old, struck me as the Energizer Bunny incarnate: moving fast and talking even faster. He also seemed remarkably thin-skinned for a public figure, prone to over-reacting to criticism of any sort.

I subsequently saw him a few times during his controversial tenure in Philadelphia, where he pushed hard for change, privatized about 40 schools, raised test scores – and spent more dollars than the city or the state wanted to.

When this proven leader accepted the challenge in 2007 to spearhead what Louisiana named the "Recovery School District" (basically the worst-performing schools in the state, most of which were in New Orleans), I was intrigued. I was already invested in the story because we'd reported from that zone three times since Hurricane Katrina and the subsequent flooding that had ravaged the schools (and everything else). Perhaps Vallas would be interested in having us follow him around, documenting his efforts. The *NewsHour* was also excited about the possibility of a strong serial that would draw in viewers.

Since Rhee and Vallas were new to their jobs, I decided to hedge my bets and call both, figuring there was no way both would agree. To have one, I believed I needed to ask two, so I called them both.

Rhee's response was, as I came to understand, direct and forceful in her typical style. "I have to figure out whether this would help me do what I have to do, which is make things better for kids. If I think it will, I will say yes. If not, I won't do it." We agreed to meet for dinner the next evening.

Then I called Paul Vallas. "Sure, come on down," he said immediately.

"We'll want complete access," I said.

"No problem."

"Do you know what you're getting yourself into in New Orleans?"

He replied that he did. "Two-thirds of the kids are at least one year older than grade level, and a large number of the kids are two years or older than grade level," he said. "I'm talking about 17-year-old eighth-graders and 18-year-old ninth-graders who are two, three, four years below grade level academically." But, he added, he also had unprecedented authority: the power to hire and fire, to change the school day and the school year, to bring in new curriculum, and so forth. Most superintendents work for a school board, but Vallas would be reporting directly to the state superintendent, a pragmatic, brainy lawyer named Paul Pastorek.

The next night Murrey Jacobson of the *NewsHour* and I took Michelle Rhee out for dinner. She asked good questions, weighed our answers and – to my great surprise – agreed to open her professional life to our cameras.

Bingo! We had access to two major school reform efforts, a coup for us. But with that elation came grim realization: We couldn't afford to cover both stories. In fact, we barely had enough to guarantee full coverage for just one year, and we knew we'd have to stick around for at least two years to see any significant educational change.

What to do? Should we choose between Rhee and Vallas? If so, whom should we follow? Both were compelling stories, both leaders had promised access, both had big plans.

It was my call, and, rather than flip a coin, I decided to gamble on a better future. We'd follow both of them, with two production teams, and I'd have to find the money somewhere.

To their credit, three foundations stepped up to the plate and allowed us to follow both stories. The Wallace Foundation, the Bill & Melinda Gates Foundation and the Eli and Edythe Broad Foundation all made grants. Not only that, they did it with a minimum of fuss, freeing us to concentrate on the work at hand.

And I can't exactly call it work – it was more of an adventure.

Michelle Rhee

Michelle A. Rhee is a Christmas baby, having arrived in Ann Arbor, Michigan, on December 25, 1969. Her parents, Shang and Inza Rhee, emigrated from South Korea in the 1960's. Raised in the Toledo, Ohio metropolitan area, she graduated from private school in 1988 and Cornell University in 1992, after which she earned a Masters in Public Policy from Harvard's Kennedy School.

She spent three years in Teach for America, teaching in a tough elementary school in Baltimore. She's told many audiences about her early failures and her eventual success in dramatically raising test scores. According to her résumé, she achieved remarkable results: moving her students from the 13th percentile to the 90th over a 2-year period.

In 1997 Rhee founded The New Teacher Project (TNTP), a non-profit organization that recruits and trains teachers for hard-to-staff schools and helps school districts reform their operations. In its first ten years, the New Teacher Project expanded to forty programs in twenty states and recruited more than 10,000 teachers. During her time at TNTP, Rhee worked closely with New York Schools Chancellor Joel Klein and the school administration in Washington.

When Adrian Fenty was elected mayor in Washington and assumed responsibility for the schools, he turned to Klein for advice about hiring a new school leader. Clearly, D.C. needed a change: 88 percent of eighth-graders had recently scored below proficient in reading on the national report card, with 93 percent below proficient in math. Without hesitation, Klein recommended Michelle Rhee. "There's a culture of mediocrity, typically, in a lot of school systems," he said. "A lot of school systems make excuses for nonperformance. And someone like Michelle, I think, can come in and, with her vision and her commitment, lead them in a different direction."

Mayor Fenty persuaded Rhee to fly out from Denver, but he had one major problem: She wasn't looking for a job.

"I told him, 'You don't want me for this job,'" said Rhee. "'You are a politician. Your job is to keep the noise to a minimum level and to keep your constituents happy.' I said, 'I am a change

111

agent, and change doesn't come without significant pushback and opposition, which is absolutely counter to what you want.'"

The mayor persisted. Finally Rhee asked, "What would you risk just for the chance to turn this school district around, to truly transform it?"

Fenty did not hesitate: "I said 'Everything,' that one word. And it's true."

In June 2007, Mayor Fenty introduced his new chancellor, who minced no words about her intentions: "I am going to run this district in a way that is constantly looking out for the best interests of the children and of the schools."

The mayor made it clear that he had her back. "We have a once-in-a-lifetime opportunity to make this school system excellent," he said. "And to the extent we can allow her to do that, as free from outside obstacles as humanly possible, the faster she will move." He told his Cabinet that he was the only person who could say "no" to her, warning them that interfering with her efforts could be a firing offense.

Paul Vallas

A proud member of the working class, Paul Vallas was raised in Roseland and Alsip, Illinois. The second oldest of four children, he and his siblings grew up working part-time jobs, usually in restaurants. Vallas says that he grew up in awe of his father, a hard-working accountant who worked all the time and expected as much from his children. "We all tried to be like him, the person he was, the worker," Paul's brother Dean told Chicago's *Catalyst Magazine.*

Paul attended parochial (Catholic and Greek Orthodox) and public schools. An indifferent student, somewhere along the way he developed a stutter, a condition he says led to his habit of speaking at what seems like a machine-gun rate. "If I slow down," he told me, "I'm likely to stutter." Paul remembered more details for *Catalyst*. "In high school I was just drifting. I was in this big, impersonal place, with my stutter and acne problems. I played on the football team, but poorly - I was the last guy on the field, if I got on the field at all. No one ever counseled me."

He ended up at Moraine Valley Community College, where he worked part time and also helped out at his father's restaurant, the Country House. And when his grades slumped, his father gave him a choice: get good grades, or get behind the grill. That bit of tough love turned his life around, Vallas remembers. "That's when I began applying myself."

He earned a BA in education and an MA in political science from Western Illinois University and taught for a year in a Greek Orthodox elementary school. Then in 1979, while working toward a second Masters degree, he caught on as a staffer for a State senator in Springfield.

Maybe his childhood fascination with sports statistics finally paid off, because he discovered an affinity for numbers and budgets. Hard working to a fault, Vallas eventually caught the eye of Chicago Mayor Daley, who made him city revenue director and then the city's Budget Director in 1994.

"We were always talking about school problems," Vallas recalled. When the state legislature gave Daley authority over the schools, he handed the job to Vallas. "He didn't offer me the job; he told me to take it." And, with the consent of his wife, Sharon, he took it.

He ran the Chicago public schools from 1995 to 2001 and the Philadelphia schools from 2002 to 2005.

Michelle Rhee

At TNTP, Rhee had supervised 120 employees. Now she would be managing – and radically changing, if things went according to plan – a school system with 55,000 students and 11,500 employees.

Rhee hit the ground running and made headlines when she toured the District's supply building. "By the time I got onto the second floor, I thought I was going to throw up," she said. "I actually felt nauseous because of what I was seeing. It was boxes and boxes of glue and scissors and composition books, binders, boxes of unopened trade books, class sets of novels, things that teachers not only are dying for but spend their own money on."

She straightened that mess out, got her 146 schools open and running on time, and then set her sights on her own central office. "You know, as I walk around, and I listen to how people operate, and I listen to the way that they answer the phone or the way they're dealing with people as they're coming to the central office, it sounds like they're very annoyed. This is not a nuisance; this is your job. So if you consider answering their questions or giving them information a nuisance, then this is not the place for you to work."

According to Joel Klein, there was only one path for Rhee to follow. "You have to get rid of people," he said. "I mean, the real fact is – she knows it, anybody who studies it knows it – there are people who are put there for patronage and other reasons and who don't really have a vital role to play. And we don't have dollars to spend on people who don't have a vital role to play."

Rhee and Fenty asked the City Council to rewrite the law to give the chancellor more leeway when it came to removing her own staff. "I need this authority for the long term to make sure that, any time there's any employee who's not producing results and who's not doing the right thing for kids, that we're able to move them out of the system," Rhee said at the time.

This made the Washington Teachers' Union and its president, George Parker, very nervous. They feared that Rhee would want more power over teachers. "The chancellor already has more than enough authority to remove from the system any teachers that are deemed ineffective or incompetent," Parker told us. "I cannot at this point imagine what additional authority the chancellor would need in order to remove ineffective teachers."

And the union had reason to be nervous. Its contract had expired, and many feared that Rhee would try to make big changes in the process used to remove ineffective teachers, the so-called "90-day plan." (This required numerous precise steps on the administration's part, and failure to follow the letter of the law aborts the process completely, requiring the administration to start all over again.)

Rhee made no secret of the value she placed on teacher quality: "I cannot risk children's education for very long while they are sitting, languishing in an ineffective teacher's classroom."

And she seemed to embrace the attention, the national spotlight. "All the eyes of the country are now on D.C.," she said. "I believe that what we are embarking upon is a fight for the lives of children." On another occasion she said, "I hope that everything that we do in some ways will have reverberations across the country."

She was also impatient. "I think what I am, is somebody who is focused on the end result that I think needs to happen," she said. "So if the rule is standing in the way of that, I will question those rules. I will bend those rules."

Bending rules wasn't required to remove school principals, so she put them on notice: Improve or else. She also gave each school leader a specific target: better test scores.

Rhee had her critics, including some veteran superintendents who felt that her emphasis on people ignored structural problems. Union president Parker sent a message: Help teachers improve; don't just make threats. He told the *NewsHour*, "We have to move the discussion away from hiring and firing of ineffective employees and begin to move the discussion to what kind of supports are we going to put in place in our district to support teachers and children."

But Rhee believed the general public was on her side: "On the weekends I'm in the grocery store. I am like in my flip-flops, and people come up to me, and they say, 'Thank goodness you're doing this. You can't do it quick enough. Don't give up.'"

Paul Vallas

Vallas also hit the ground running, full of confidence. He had, after all, managed two large districts and was now in charge of just 13,000 students, only 60 schools – and no tough teachers union to deal with. Given the size of the district, Vallas predicted improvements: "I think the institutional framework can be laid here within the next two years, and I think we can start seeing results within the next year or so."

How confident was he? "If within two years this district has not significantly improved," he said, "if I have not achieved 90 percent of what I've promised then they should put me on the Amtrak and send me back home to Chicago."

Like Michelle Rhee in Washington, Vallas has boundless energy. "My day will usually begin about 7:30 in the morning, particularly if I'm doing a school visit," he said. "An early day for me is 6:30, a late day for me ends at 9:30, 10 o'clock."

Educationally, New Orleans schools were terrible even before Katrina. On one state test, for instance, 80 percent of students were below basic on math, 88 percent below basic in English. Many schools not badly damaged by Katrina and the flooding were already falling apart. Parents who could afford private or parochial school took their children out of the public system, and most of Vallas' new students were living in poverty or near-poverty.

Vallas had a plan. He gave parents a laundry list of physical improvements he wanted to see in the still-devastated city: air-conditioned classrooms with proper lighting, modern furniture, up-to-date textbooks, a benchmarked instructional program, regular testing and modern technology – including laptops for all high school students.

Veteran teachers were skeptical. "He is bright-eyed. I know he's been successful elsewhere, but New Orleans is different," one high school teacher told us. "He doesn't understand the reality. He doesn't have to deal with the logistics of the laptop when it gets stolen."

Vallas dismissed her criticism as negativity. "I suggest that teacher look for another school district because that's the exact low expectations that we set for inner-city kids, and that's the same attitude that resulted in many inner-city districts deciding that children shouldn't take textbooks home, because they'll lose the textbooks," he said.

In Vallas' view, low expectations all but guarantee low performance. "A lot of time when you raise expectations, people say you're being naïve, but it's like what comes first, the chicken or the egg? What comes first, the low performance or the low expectations?" For him, the question is rhetorical. Low expectations produce poor results.

Like Michelle Rhee, Vallas believes that good teachers are the foundation. "There's no substitute for that enthusiastic teacher who's willing to work like there's no tomorrow," he said.

That's why he invested heavily in Teach For America, recruiting as many corps members as he could. "What they bring to the classroom are content mastery, enthusiasm and unbelievable work ethic, very high expectations for kids, high expectations for success and a sense of optimism," he said. Vallas also loved their willingness to work. "They don't punch a clock. They're not 9 to 4, they're not five days a week. They really commit themselves and throw themselves into the job."

But Vallas didn't dictate to his principals about their hiring practices, meaning that Cheryllyn Branche was free to hire the teachers she wanted at Benjamin Banneker Elementary School. "I prefer people who know what they're doing. I prefer people who have a proven track record. I prefer people who are going to stay here and work with our children for the long haul," Ms. Branche said. In other words, no one from Teach For America need apply.

Vallas wanted dedication above all. What sort of teachers ought to be worried about their jobs, I asked him. "If you have poor attendance, if you have low expectations for children, if you're showing up at school five minutes before the school day begins and you're leaving school five minutes after the school day ends, I think you should probably be a little nervous," he said.

Vallas has had to deal with different perceptions on the part of some of his teachers, who seem to expect little from their students. "You have kids who don't think education is important. You have kids who come from families who don't push the issue about getting to school on time or even getting to school at all," one teacher told us. From her perspective, the problem was "the apathy in the home/community environment."

Even if Vallas held that view, his response would be to attack the problem. "The challenge for us is to try to compensate for what's missing at home. And that means you keep the schools open longer. You provide the children with three meals a day. You expand the number of social services that you can provide," he said.

At faculty convocation just before school opened, Vallas rallied his troops, telling them that, by dedicating themselves to the education of young people, they were part of "the greatest chapter in the American civil rights movement."

"You will set that bar, you will raise that bar," he exhorted. "You will set those high expectations."

The teachers cheered, but, unfortunately, the students didn't get the message. On opening day, about 40 percent stayed home.

Michelle Rhee

Early in her first year, Rhee had to confront a deficit of $100 million. Her response? "We spend more per pupil than almost any other urban jurisdiction does, and that's partially because we have a lot of our resources and money going into facilities that are a quarter-full or a half-full." She was right. Enrollment in D.C. had dropped by 27 percent in the previous 10 years, and two-dozen or more schools were significantly under-enrolled. Her solution: to immediately close 15 percent of the buildings. When that news leaked, the City Council was furious.

Rhee held community meetings to hear complaints and explain her thinking, but she refused to consider group decision-making or consensus-building. "If the leader of the school district went about closing schools by saying, 'What does everyone think about this? How do you think we should do it?' I would lose faith immediately in that person," she said.

Mayor Fenty agreed: "By definition, if she had done that, it would no longer have been the plan to make the schools excellent. Before you even started, it would have already been compromised."

Rhee showed her willingness – some say her eagerness – to embrace confrontation. "Bottom line is, I'm not going to get to a point where everybody agrees on one decision. No matter what decision we make in the end, some group of people is going to be unhappy. I can guarantee you that."

As opposition grew, Rhee had the support of the only person who really mattered: Mayor Adrian Fenty. And he made his wishes perfectly clear: "People say, 'You're moving too fast; you're trying to push too much right now.' ... But when you're out in the neighborhoods of the District of Columbia talking to regular people, they're saying, 'Go faster. Fix things. Do more.'"

In the end, Rhee announced that six of the 23 schools she'd intended to close would be spared, but added four new ones to the list.

Paul Vallas

He may have inherited a small district compared to his previous Chicago and Philadelphia posts, but New Orleans had, and has, major problems – and Vallas knew it. "There's drug deals going on, drive-by shootings. The violence that we face in our communities is tied to poverty and tied to educational failure and things of this nature," he said.

Educational failure was rampant. At one point, 85 percent of New Orleans students were scoring below basic on state tests. "This is a very tough job," he said. "This is a very tough environment. We're educating kids that are way behind. All the kids are at least one, two, three years below grade level. That's really a challenge."

My impression of Paul Vallas is that he is willing to try just about anything – and everything – if there's even the slightest chance it will make a difference. And if something isn't working, he'll pull the plug, even though he may not be willing to admit that he made a mistake.

Vallas embraced "smart boards," which allow a teacher to project material from a laptop computer. Early on, he promised laptop computers for all high school students, and, when they were distributed, he described the plan to a group of local clergy. "That simple act, putting that computer in the hands of that child and allowing that child to take that computer home was our statement of confidence and optimism about the potential of that child," he said. "That's what it's about."

Still, he couldn't help boasting to the clergy about his students. The computer experts had told him that the laptops were set up so students couldn't access the Internet, but "it took the kids 20 minutes to hack into the computers," he said. "Just 20 minutes. Don't tell me that our inner-city kids are not the brightest kids on the block, because they are."

With nearly unlimited power to change schedules, Vallas instituted an extended day program and an extended year. Many schools now run past 5 p.m., and the school year, which begins in August, continues into the following July.

"The game plan is to get the elementary school kids up to grade level. And to get them up to grade level at an accelerated pace," Vallas said, adding that children will spend four hours a day on reading, language arts, comprehension and vocabulary, and two hours a day on mathematics. He nearly jumped out of his chair to make the next point. "There is an absolute direct correlation between the amount of instructional time on task and student progress."

Paul Vallas' greatest challenge is an ugly tradition of school failure: a deep belief that public schools just don't work. If a young person grows up knowing that going to school didn't do much for either his parents or his grandparents, how much faith should he have in schools? Outside of Vallas' enthusiasm, we saw, again and again, a pattern of indifference. The following conversation with some high school students captures it well:

ME: A lot of students don't show up on a Friday? Why is that?
YOUNG MAN: It's kind of like Friday doesn't matter because most teachers don't really give a lot of work that day. It's kind of like a half day to relax.
YOUNG WOMAN: Because it's just a half day, some people want to get their weekend early.
ANOTHER YOUNG WOMAN: They want an early weekend.
ME: Sounds like you're saying Friday is part of the weekend.
YOUNG MAN: Most likely.

121

ME: But a lot of kids also skip school on Monday. Why is that?
YOUNG WOMAN: They don't come on Monday because Sunday they didn't get any rest, so they rest on Monday.

When Paul Vallas arrived in New Orleans, he set about the task of rebuilding a broken school system. He tore down ruined buildings and spent millions refurbishing damaged ones. He truly believed in that cliché from the movie *Field of Dreams*: If you build it, they will come.

So far that has not been true, but Vallas wasn't giving up. "It is a serious problem but I'm not going to change to accommodate the culture. I want the culture to change to accommodate me," he said.

Michelle Rhee

Trouble was brewing on the labor relations front, especially after the City Council gave Rhee authority to fire central office staff at will – which she used to fire 98 employees (over 10 percent of the staff).

The teachers union, whose contract had expired, was nervous. "There are many who feel that they can transform education by simply focusing on children and supporting children. You have to support those who interact daily with children, our teachers, if you're going to get the results," Union President George Parker said hopefully, even as the chancellor and her staff were taking hard-line positions about D.C.'s teaching force.

Michelle Rhee has a comic's timing and a politician's gift for phrasemaking, a combination that has occasionally gotten her into trouble. For example, she didn't help her cause when she said this to us: "People now are beginning to cast me as heartless – 'Fire everybody, get rid of everybody.' That is not, in and of itself, the answer in isolation." (And here she paused.) "But it's a good start."

Was the chancellor anti-union?

"Let me say this," replied Parker. "Her statements in the past have not been very favorable to unions."

When Rhee first met her teachers in August 2007, she was supportive. "There is no one that I would rather have on my team leading this, as the people in this room," she told them. But six months later her tune had changed. "There will be some schools where a significant amount of the teaching force will turn over," she told us. "I think that we are going to need a different breed of educators."

We asked what a "significant amount" meant. Rhee's director of professional development, Cheryl Krehbiel, was candid. "Fifty percent don't have the right mindset," she told us. "And there's the possibility that more of them don't have the content knowledge to do the job."

Some school principals agreed. L. Nelson Burton, principal of Coolidge High School, said: "It's a terrible thing to say, but half of the staff here ought not be. They just don't fit into what we're doing here. And I dare say many of them won't fit into any program where we're trying to raise student achievement."

Did it surprise the chancellor to hear one of her principals say, "I wish I could fire half my teachers. They're not on board. They're not effective"?

Her response was typically blunt: "Does it surprise me? No. I've heard things like that from lots of principals."

But principals like Burton had the means to remove ineffective teachers: the 90-day plan. They can give teachers notice, provide help over a 90-day period, and then remove them if they don't show improvement. At the time, Burton had only four of his teachers on the 90-day plan. The union's Parker was quick to criticize: "If you're telling me half of your staff is not living up to par, the next question I want to ask you, as a leader, talk to me about what you've done to try to develop that staff."

Rhee made no secret of her desire for a new breed of teacher: men and women who thought the way she had when she was in the classroom. As she said, "we have to have people who are willing to take personal responsibility and to say, despite all of the obstacles that are currently in the way of our kids – because there are tremendous obstacles – if you're not willing to say, 'But despite all those things, I'm going to make sure that my kids are going to succeed at the highest levels,' then this might not be the district for you."

And she was confident that her kind of teachers were out there. "I get emails from people across the country who want to come and work for us. There are a lot of people who are very excited about what we're doing."

She also wanted to revolutionize the way teachers are paid, tying wages to student performance. As discussed previously, most contracts base pay on years served and graduate credits earned. And like Bill Gates, Rhee found this absurd.

She had a distinct advantage in the negotiations because the union was losing members to charter schools. At the time, more than 25 percent of D.C. students were attending charters. To stop the loss, Parker said, the union had to pay attention to student learning. "Normally, unions have not had to contend with any sense of accountability or responsibility for student achievement, and our existence and survival has not depended upon that," he told us. Now it was, he said, a "bread and butter issue" for teachers.

Rhee put a bold two-tiered proposal on the table, offering teachers the chance to earn six-figure salaries if their students did well. But there was a catch: Tenured teachers would have to give up job security for a year. Then, if their students did well, they got the money and got their tenure back. But if not, they could lose their jobs.

In D.C., a 10-year veteran with a master's degree was earning just over $64,000. Under Rhee's two-tiered proposal, teachers could stick with that approach, the so-called "red path," and get step raises.

But if teachers chose the pay for performance model (the "green path"), and if their students performed well, that 10-year veteran could earn as much as $122,000 in salary and bonuses.

Parker said that most of his members opposed Rhee's plan, and Rhee said she would push back hard. Then she issued what sounded like a take-it-or-leave-it offer: "And the bottom line is that the union is going to have to decide whether they're going to accept my final offer and we're going to roll this out in a tentative agreement or not." And, she added, whether the plan passed or not, she would find ways to remove ineffective teachers.

Negotiations stalled, and the chancellor's prominence became an issue, particularly when she appeared on the cover of *TIME* magazine, posed in an empty classroom with a broom in her hand.

George Parker did not mince words: "It created a culture of low morale, one that was the lowest that I've seen since I've been in D.C. public schools, and I've been here for 25 years."

Some teachers agreed, saying that students were now openly disrespecting them. "There will be students who will start your day off saying, 'Oh, yeah, I've read the article. You all are getting fired anyway,'" said Randy Brown, a ninth-grade English teacher. "And they absolutely believe it. You can't really be accountable when you're undermined. They don't believe in you. They've lost their confidence in their teachers."

Had Rhee's criticism of some teachers alienated others to such a degree that a contract was beyond reach? Parker felt it had. "The morale is so low it would be very difficult to have folks truly buy into where you want to go and ride the train, because if folks

125

are feeling that, 'Look, they're just waiting to throw me off the train,' that it's going to be very difficult for me to ride it."

In response, Rhee said she wanted to help her teachers succeed. She increased the budget for professional development to almost $20 million, about five times greater than before. She also provided most schools with new staff whose job it was to help teachers improve.

She told us that more support for teachers and better teamwork were among her priorities for the district, and then – not for the first time – she blamed the press. "A lot of the things that were coming out in the press were sort of saying, you know, 'Rhee wants to fire people. It's all about firing people.' And I don't think that it was a comprehensive sort of view of what I actually believe," she said.

At one point during her second year, Rhee launched an effort to speak directly to teachers, holding meetings after school where teachers could ask her anything. She called them "listening sessions." We were not allowed to watch these, but the reviews were, at best, mixed. Most of the teachers we spoke with said Rhee did most of the talking.

Negotiations came to a halt during the summer of 2009, when Rhee's principals dismissed 239 teachers, even though the system had hired over 900 for the coming year. This situation required a "reduction in force," or RIF. Because Rhee tied the layoffs to budget pressures, she was not bound by the existing teachers' contract. To make the reduction in force, principals used a formula devised by Rhee, in which seniority counted for just 5 percent.

Some charged that Rhee had deliberately over-hired so she could then fire teachers she deemed ineffective. The national union, the American Federation of Teachers, stepped up its involvement, tempers blazed and the matter went to court. Rhee was adamant when she appeared before the City Council. "My understanding is that I do have the authority, as the agency head, to make the decisions about moving budget from one place to another," she testified.

The courts agreed, and the firings were not reversed. How much damage that did to the chancellor's standing with her teachers was impossible to calculate.

During the session, Councilmember Michael Brown asked Rhee: "You clearly don't trust a lot of the stakeholders. It's obvious the stakeholders don't trust your office. So, how do we repair this?"

"I will fully do my part, to the extent that people have suggestions about how we move forward," she responded. "Some of the difficult decisions that we make will indeed cause some people to be unhappy. But we know we have to push forward on those decisions because they are right for schools and kids."

Paul Vallas

Whatever else he may accomplish in New Orleans, Paul Vallas is likely to be remembered – and mostly celebrated – for his enthusiastic embrace of charter schools. On his watch, the Recovery School District has become the most heavily chartered district in the nation, and Vallas predicts that before he leaves every school will either have a charter or be what he calls "charter-like," meaning that most of the authority rests at the school level.

His support is philosophical. "I'm a believer in schools having the freedom and autonomy to make decisions that are in the best interest of the children. And so I support charter schools, because charter schools are a vehicle for achieving that type of freedom," he said.

Vallas' support of charters is also political. While he can recommend that failing schools become charters, the final decision is up to State Superintendent Paul Pastorek. Here the two

Pauls share a goal: Keep the old New Orleans School Board, infamous for its corruption, patronage and academic failure, from returning to power. Here's how Paul Vallas explains it: "My goal is to make sure that within the next two to three years we will have a system of schools that are independent of the old damaging covenants that existed prior to the hurricane. And that is a top-down management control structure that limits your ability to hire the best people and fire the worst people, that limits your ability to have a longer school day and longer school year, that keeps you from doing things in the best interests of the kids."

He likes the idea of decentralized authority. So do his principals, including Sharon Clark. "As principal of a charter school you are responsible for everything," she said. "I make sure instruction is in place and it's effective and aligned with the state standards. I make sure that the budget is balanced and that we have money for payroll. I make sure that we continue to register kids and that our attendance works." Her school, Sophie B. Wright Middle School, was failing until Vallas made it into a charter. Now it's wildly successful, with parents petitioning Vallas to let the school add another grade – so their children won't have to leave to go to a regular high school.

Not everyone was enthusiastic about Vallas' grand design. Cheryllyn Branche, principal of Benjamin Banneker Elementary (one of the most improved schools in the district), says she spurned Vallas' invitation to become a charter school. "I think there are good charters and bad charters," she told us. "I really do feel that there's room at the table, but I don't think to designate that the entire city be 'charterized' makes any sense. Good schools make sense for every child."

What troubles Branche is how some charter schools treat children with special needs. She believes some schools are pushing these children away – which is illegal – and are doing it in subtle ways. "Parents are seeking places for their children who may have physical handicaps, mental or emotional handicapping conditions and they're not being accepted by charters," she said. Instead, she said, parents report that charter school principals recommend enrolling the child at Banneker: "Go to Banneker, tell Miss Branche I sent you. Go to Banneker."

Vallas denies that "dumping" – the common term – is going on, but he's sharpened his eye nonetheless. Here's how he explains it: "Charters are generally much smaller than regular traditionally run schools, so charters may not have the capacity to have the various specialties like the speech therapists, etc. A parent's going to ask, 'Do you have these services?' And if the charter doesn't have those services, the parent's going to look for another school."

Vallas is splitting hairs here, because a parent is entitled by law to enroll a child at the school of his or her choice, and the school is then obligated to provide the necessary services. Is that blatant discrimination? Parent advocate Karran Harper Royal doesn't mince words: "That's discrimination. You can dress it up however you'd like to, but it's really discrimination."

While Vallas denies the charge, he is moving to create ways for charter schools to share the cost of expensive services like special education. He recognizes that decentralization can provide opportunities for misbehavior and worse, and so he's promised to be on guard. "As more of our schools are granted charter-like independence, we're going to be doing more policing," he said. "We're going to focus more on accountability. And if a school is deliberately discouraging people or turning people away, that would be breach of contract, and it could lose its charter."

Vallas continues to encourage and create charter schools. In the 2010-11 school year, two-thirds of his schools were operating under their own charters. It's an unprecedented 'natural experiment,' and one that anyone interested in public education must pay attention to.

129

Michelle Rhee

She is a wonderful interview, smart and engaging and honest, perhaps to a fault. At one point I asked her if she had any regrets about any of her actions. She paused for a moment and then said, "You know, I'm a very unusual person in that, in my entire life, I don't have any regrets."

And, she noted, she couldn't be happier. "I'm living what I think education reformers and parents throughout this country have long hoped for, which is somebody who will just come in, and do the things that they felt were right, and everything else be damned."

On another occasion, I asked her about her leadership style: specifically, if she saw herself as a benevolent dictator.

"Maybe," she said with a smile.

"'Dictator' is OK?"

"If by 'dictator,' you mean somebody who, at the end of the day, is fully comfortable being held accountable for, you know, the results and is going to be incredibly decisive about the direction that we're heading in," she replied, "then yes."

The Washington schools have shown improvement on her watch. In fall 2009, math scores on the prestigious NAEP test, known as "The Nation's Report Card," were released. Although Washington's scores remain lowest in the nation, only D.C. and four states saw gains at both levels tested: fourth and eighth grades, and Washington was the *only* urban district to show such gains. (However, the elementary level scores on the local test, DC-CAS, declined in the spring of 2010, which Rhee's opponents seized on as evidence that her test-prep regimen is counter-productive.)

The so-called "Red and Green" plan never made it into the contract, but, in the end, Rhee, George Parker and Randi Weingarten hammered out a deal that gave the chancellor even more authority. Seniority privileges are weaker than ever before, and teacher evaluations are tied directly to student performance. When the contract was finally put to a vote, over 80 percent of teachers approved—although the turnout was surprisingly low. The carrot for teachers was an immediate raise, retroactive to the date the previous contract expired—three years ago. Clearly, the prospect of that one large chunk of cash attracted a landslide vote in favor of the deal.

Lost in the clamor was the fact that this supposed 5-year contract was 3/5 over the instant it was signed, because it was retroactive to 2007. That means that negotiations must begin again in 2011, because this contract expires in 2012.

As for Rhee, she said from the beginning that she intended to stay as long as the mayor wanted her to, by which she meant eight years. She had assumed, as had many others early in Fenty's term, that he would win reelection; after all, he had carried every ward the first time around.

But Rhee's plans for an 8-year all out school reform crusade came crashing down on September 14th, 2010, when Adrian Fenty lost the Democratic nomination for mayor to City Council President Vincent Gray, a career politician known for being cautious to a fault. Frustrated with what he perceived to be Fenty's (and Rhee's) aloofness and arrogance, Gray built a war chest, ran a masterful campaign—and routed Fenty.

The following evening Rhee publicly called the election results "a disaster for the children of Washington," effectively ending any chance of her continuing as Chancellor.

She and Gray met several times, and on October 13th Rhee announced her resignation, effective October 30.

Within days she had her own Twitter account, with 5,000 followers soon after it appeared, a Facebook page, and - according to Joel Klein - at least 60 job offers.

And after D.C., what's next? Rhee was not saying, except to reiterate her initial position: "This is my first and only superintendent's job."

My takeaway from spending this time with Michelle Rhee is that she is very comfortable in her own skin, secure in her belief in accountability and measurement. She's a bottom-line leader who believes in what can be measured, and she's willing to use any carrots and sticks necessary to get results.

She has said it herself on many occasions: "The bottom line is that, yes, everybody who works for me has to feel comfortable and know that at the end of the day we're going to look at the results. And if the results are not there, if they are not producing significant gains for kids, then there is a chance that they won't be here in the long term."

"So it is really 'Produce or you're out?'" I asked.

"Shouldn't it be?" she shot back.

Shouldn't it be? Her question is a potent reminder that, whatever she does next, Michelle Rhee won a major victory, both in Washington and nationally. Simply put, she reframed the debate about how teachers are paid. Largely because of her, it's no longer possible to argue convincingly that teachers, whether effective or not, should be paid based on their years on the job and graduate credits earned. Largely because of her, it's impossible not to recognize the absurdity of the current system. Largely because of her, George Parker and the Washington Teachers' Union, Randi Weingarten of the American Federation of Teachers, and the Obama administration's Race to the Top program all acknowledge that, somehow, teacher evaluation must be based on student performance.

What formulas will be used, how heavily test scores will count and how well the new approaches will work – all that is yet to be determined.

And that's not the only significant change she's responsible for. As mentioned previously, her teacher evaluation system, known as IMPACT, grades teachers on a 1-4 scale, with student performance counting for half of the score in tested grades. Every teacher is to be observed five times during the course of the year, and teachers scoring a 1, the lowest level, will be dismissed, regardless of tenure. That too is revolutionary, and in the summer of 2010, Rhee announced that 241 teachers, about 5% of the teaching force, would be dismissed, 165 for poor performance. Those scoring close to 4 are supposed to receive significant bonuses. Rhee was able to impose the evaluation system without bargaining with the union because of D.C.'s unique status in the American system. Basically, the Congress gives her unprecedented power.

Rhee's deputy chancellor, Kaya Henderson, was named to succeed her on an interim basis. Everyone is watching closely to see if Gray pulls back from Rhee's reforms—he won with the strong support of the teachers unions, both local and national, and the unions generally detest the idea of connecting test scores with teacher evaluation and pay.

Rhee has moved on. In December 2010, she announced the creation of Students First, and she did it with great fanfare: on Oprah and the cover of *Newsweek*. Her modest goals: 'transform public education,' raise one billion dollars, and attract one million members!

Paul Vallas

At times, Paul Vallas seemed to be trying to position himself as the opposite of Michelle Rhee, particularly when it came to the question of firing people. When I asked him if he thought he would be replacing many of his principals, he smiled. "Well, I don't know if I anticipate replacing a lot," he said. "We'll probably replace some, but I'm not going to parade out principals or teachers or give you a body count." He paused, and then went on, "You need to be careful that you're not grandstanding and that you're not alienating your rank and file."

Vallas seems congenitally unable to either slow down or dwell on negativity. Once while we were riding in his car to a school, he got into a phone conversation with his boss, Superintendent Paul Pastorek. I heard him say, more than once, that he must have been crazy to take this job. Later in an interview I asked him if he'd ever regretted coming to New Orleans.

"Never!"

I reminded him of what he'd said that morning on the phone to Pastorek. His response: "I was just commiserating, trying to cheer him up."

And when he's having a bad day? "It's usually for a good reason," he said. "And that just means I intensify my efforts. We've got a steep hill to climb."

Vallas has made progress. Scores on state tests have gone up every year, but he's not satisfied. As he puts it: "I say that we're just at base camp preparing to climb Mount Everest. But last year we weren't even in the Himalayas."

When he signed on in New Orleans, Paul Vallas made it clear that he was staying for only two years, and no longer. Then he re-upped for the third year, which he did with all sorts of political rumors about a possible run for state-wide office in Illinois swirling around his head. While he stayed for a fourth year, he has made clear that he has his next project in his sights: helping rebuild schools in Haiti. Admittedly ambitious and still youthful and energetic at 57, Vallas admits to thinking occasionally about what might have been. He lost the Democratic nomination for governor of Illinois by a tiny margin to the since-disgraced Rod Blagojevich and, when he was in charge of the Chicago schools, he hired Arne Duncan, the man who became President Obama's secretary of education.

The pattern in school districts rarely varies. A new superintendent comes in, shakes things up and tries to build a strong system that will continue after he or she leaves: a monument, in effect. That rarely happens, precisely because the next man or woman follows the same path of dismantling and rebranding.

New Orleans will be a different story. Whether he leaves now or stays on, Paul Vallas has created a new model for running schools. His Recovery School District is very close to being "a system of schools," and not "a school system," which is his avowed goal. Challenges remain. If he can create a strong oversight mechanism to keep charter schools on track, if he can develop economies of scale for costly services like special education, if he can identify and train his successor and if he can convince the downtrodden half of New Orleans that this new public education system exists for their benefit, then Paul Vallas' legacy in New Orleans will be secure – and the "system of schools" will be working so well that his successors will work to improve it, not reinvent things.

11

The School Turnaround
Specialist

In its never-ending search for quick, preferably inexpensive cures, public education has latched onto the notion of the Turnaround Specialist. It was the hot idea in education in 2004, the brainchild of then Virginia governor (now senator) Mark Warner, who was a venture capitalist and successful businessman before he entered politics. Former governor Warner wanted to create a training program that would turn successful principals into the equivalent of the turnaround managers he had seen work wonders in the business arena.

Turning around schools, and the specialists who make it happen, are hot ideas again. In fact, 'turning around' troubled schools was one of the four so-called pillars of the Department of Education's Race to the Top competition for $4.35 billion in federal discretionary funds. Education Secretary Arne Duncan embraced the turnaround concept when he led Chicago's public schools, and today he's calling for a cadre of "warrior principals" to fix failing schools.

Back in 2004, Virginia was the leader, with a program based at the University of Virginia involving both the school of education and the business school. What began as a summer institute has grown into a two-year program that is developing a jargon all its own. For instance, educators in participating districts who work with those training to become turnaround specialists are known as "shepherds." Virginia's turnaround program is unabashedly pro-business, emphasizing the techniques of good management and the bottom line of test scores over pedagogy. As its website notes, those chosen for the program receive "the type of executive education typically received only by top-level business leaders."

Today other states and districts are on the bandwagon, with the federal government leading the band.

However, I suggest you hold your applause. Covering the story for *NewsHour*, my colleagues and I spent a year with one of Virginia's turnaround specialists at a school in Richmond, Virginia, and what I saw makes me wary of this approach. Parker Land, a successful principal for nine years at a high school in suburban Virginia, just outside of Washington, was chosen for the second cadre of turnaround specialists. We followed him throughout his training and his first year as principal of a troubled urban middle school in Richmond, the state capital. We produced four segments for the *NewsHour*, pieces that have relevance today.

Idealistic and restless, Land, then in his mid-50s, took a pay cut to join the program. After the training, he was put in charge of Thomas C. Boushall Middle School and its 735 students. Boushall was on a state warning list, put there by a nearly 50 percent failure rate in reading. It had gone through three principals in seven years, and the year before Land arrived the staff had issued some 2,500 infractions for student misconduct.

Warm and engaging, Land was open about his reason for taking on this challenge. "I truly believe that if we don't solve the problems of inner-city schools, our democracy is going to suffer," he said.

His new boss, Richmond superintendent Deborah Jewell-Sherman, was confident Land would be successful. "I believe he is tough enough. I believe he has the commitment. I think he'll be able to inspire his staff with a 'can do' spirit."

Land was equally confident. "It's not a huge mystery as to how to turn schools around. It's leadership, establishing a basic understanding of respect among all parties, and that includes students." Land saw the school passing the state test for the first time. And by the end of the year, he predicted, Boushall itself would be transformed. "I see a school that sparkles. I see student work everywhere, everywhere. I see smiles. I hear joy."

"Are you a missionary?" I asked.

"One of the things I really don't want to sound like is a missionary," he replied. "I do not want to sound like a missionary. But I have a mission."

"He may not like that word," his superintendent said, "but the one thing I can't teach anyone is to love the kids and believe in them and move any mountain to get the best for those students. Some call it fire in the belly, some call it passion, but whatever you call it, he has it."

Land, who is white, brought the best of intentions and 31 years of experience in public education to his new school, where three out of four students were living in poverty and nearly all were African-American. The new environment didn't scare him. "I have been able to create a kind of an expectation in the schools I've worked in that improvement is the norm. Change is the norm."

But that was in the comfortable suburbs. We walked through Boushall with Land a few days before it officially opened, and he pointed to many of its physical deficiencies – broken clocks, dirty windows, and shades that didn't work – but what upset him most was the way students were greeted. "I don't like the fact that the first thing a kid does when he walks in the building is have to go through a metal detector. One of my personal goals is that we won't have to do that for very much longer," he

138

told us. "What I want to get across to kids is that this is a real caring environment and it's a helping environment."

Maybe so, but to get into that caring environment, kids had to take off their outer clothing and pass through metal detectors. Some were frisked by a cadre of security officers immediately after shaking the hand of their new principal.

On the first morning, Land was taken aback. "I was not prepared for the pandemonium at that entry area," he said. "It's all due to the fact that we have to get all those kids through the metal detector. I just wasn't used to that. I wasn't prepared for that."

His approach was to get to know as many students as possible and to engage them at their level. One day they asked him about his new role.

"What is a turnover teacher?" a student asked.

"Actually, my title is a turnaround specialist, but all I am is a principal," Land said.

"What kind of training did you have to go through to become a turnaround specialist?" a different student asked.

"I had to go to about two weeks of classes on all kinds of different things, like how to set goals and objectives for staff, how to work through problems, those kinds of things."

"How long do you plan on working as a principal?"

"I plan on working as a principal for at least three more years and I hope to be here longer than that."

The turnaround specialist program required a three-year commitment from all participants. "My commitment is three years," said Land. "I tell everybody that."

We learned Land's management philosophy pretty early on the first day, when he saw how many kids were roaming the halls. This, he told us, was the responsibility of teachers. In fact, we learned that in his worldview, most school problems traced back to the same source. "So much of misbehavior is a result of teachers just being poorly planned," he said.

Clearly he intended to take a hard line: "I am trying to get across in everything I do that the teacher is accountable. The teacher is accountable for every kid who is out in the hall and for every kid that's asleep in their class – all those things."

Did he really believe that bad behavior was a consequence of bad teaching? His response was firm: "You can preclude a lot of student misbehavior with a good lesson plan."

A seventh-grader agreed. "A lot of students don't pay attention in class because I don't think the teachers are putting forth effort to make us feel interested in class. If they had more activities and more fun things to do in class, 90 percent of us would be doing our work."

Was that analysis – it's essentially all on the teachers – overly simplistic? A veteran teacher suspected Land was not aware of Boushall's reality. "He's walking into a school that, for one thing, is not fully accredited," English teacher Madieth Malone told us. "He's walking into a school that is predominantly black. He's walking into a situation that, unfortunately, is surrounded by very low-income housing. He's walking into a typical inner-city school."

Malone had her own analysis of the challenge: "In order for him to be a turnaround specialist the way I understand turnaround specialists, he has to turn around the attitudes that teachers have, he has to turn around parents' attitudes, and he has to turn the attitudes of the community as they perceive our school family. He has a lot of turning around to do."

Soon Land's idealism was put to the test, the first of many tests, as it turned out. Kids were fighting, pushing and shoving, and Land himself had to grapple with a seventh-grader, who nearly pushed him to the ground.

Just a month into the year, he was candid about the lack of progress. "I can't stand failure. And it feels like failure, is what it feels like." But he continued to believe that teachers were the key to a successful turnaround. "I see the bigger picture. I'm working on discipline. You cannot separate classroom management, behavior management and good instruction," he told us.

Teachers were skeptical. "To me, that is the utopia-type situation you want to have," math teacher Lois Smith said, "but come on. We need some reality here."

Reality turned out to be a string of daily fights and a wakeup call for Land. "One I had to actually break up myself with a security guard," he acknowledged. "I was on the floor, trying to get kids apart, and it was pretty ugly."

Reluctantly Land dropped the strategy he'd announced to teachers at the beginning of the school year, that good instruction was *the* solution to bad behavior. Now he had a new plan, he told his teachers: "Solid rules, solid consequences, solid rewards. That's a program."

Lois Smith was not persuaded. "I'm not sure if he really knew what he was getting into," she told us. "I don't know if he realized what the inner-city student was like."

Land didn't entirely disagree. "I have lots of experience with kids who have real tough environments and abusive environments, and those emotional issues, and those kind of needs that prevent them from learning. But it's the sheer number that's here; that was something I wasn't prepared for."

But when Land asked teachers to buy into his new plan, which included having them monitor the halls and stay after school to run detention hall as ways of bringing control to Boushall, he hit a wall. Teachers who had been told that their teaching was the problem were now unwilling to become the solution.

141

It was a compelling scene: the principal asking plaintively, "What do you all think? I need to know. What's the commitment?" and getting nothing but blank stares in return.

A teacher told us later that Land should show them the money. "They feel fine, as long as they can get paid," said Thaddeus Smith. In fact, Boushall teachers were earning on average $11,000 a year less than teachers in the suburbs.

"We have a lot of teachers that have other responsibilities, other jobs and things like that," Mr. Smith continued. "If we have to stay after school, can we get some funds for it? Unfortunately, we didn't have that. You know, even though it's for the benefit or the betterment of the school, money talks and everything else walks."

Land became a disciplinarian. He moved disruptive students to split up cliques, and suspended others, sending them to a trailer (called "Choices") used by previous principals to keep troublemakers out of the way.

One of his supervisors was not impressed. She told him: "We're going to need to look at your plan for remediation recovery because if you look at your writing scores, they were not good. We're going to have to be on it, and we're going to have to be very vigilant; we see things that are not going in the direction we want them to go." She seemed to be telling him that spending so much time on discipline was taking away from instructional time.

Seventh-graders had a better grasp of reality. "There was basically a fight every single day; it was fight after fight after fight," one student told us.

Another echoed her complaint: "I was heading to my locker, and I heard somebody say, "Hit him!" And then I turned around, and they were getting them serious faces, and I knew I had to get out of there."

After we witnessed another day of constant fighting, Land suspended *us*! No more cameras to document his struggles for a national audience, although he promised he'd invite us back "once things settled down."

Boushall was noticeably quieter when he let us back in, four months later. "We've reduced the fighting, but not to the point where anybody feels that we're successful. The tendencies are there, but I think what you're seeing is more of a calmness," Land said.

He had created a system of positive rewards, including after-school dances and ice cream socials for students with good attendance. "I believe that kids respond to positive rewards," he said. "We're going to stroke our kids who do their homework, who don't cut class and all the kinds of things that we know make kids successful in school."

Of course these are tried-and-true strategies used in schools everywhere, not discoveries from the world of business.

Land provided his own analysis: "In a sense, there's a turnaround going on here. There really is. But the term 'turnaround' kind of connotes something dramatic, you know? But I don't know if it's so dramatic. I don't think it's going to be that dramatic. I think it's little victories that you win on a daily basis."

"Are you, then, a gradual turnaround specialist?" I asked.

"Maybe so," he said. "We'll see."

His boss, Superintendent Deborah Jewell-Sherman, wasn't into gradualism. "I have serious 'come to the woodshed' conversations about my expectations," she said. "I want that school fully accredited."

And the key to accreditation was test scores.

Teachers changed their routine. "A lot of time is being spent on how to take tests, what kinds of questions are on tests, how to read test questions, the facts that are needed to answer questions on a test," English teacher Madieth Malone told us. "We usually spend time reading novels. I would love to do that, but now I need to spend my time focused on the bare necessities, those absolute things that I know will be tested."

In Lois Smith's math classes, test prep had taken over. "The goal is that they've got to pass the test. Some of the kids aren't going to learn all the concepts, but if they have some of the strategies, they still can pass."

And so she taught strategies, not mathematical concepts.

Malone was upset. "I can't go along with that, no. I can't support that. The goal for all of our schools – and I guess it's the goal for schools across the country – is to pass standardized tests, but the goal of educators is to prepare children to become responsible, contributing adults."

Land accepted the compromise. "There's so much more to these kids that needs to be developed, but the educational world says, 'Show me academic test scores.' That's life now. So that's the way it's going to be."

After the testing and a few days before school ended, Land had a surprise announcement. His promise of a three-year commitment was null and void. He was leaving Boushall.

"It was out of the blue," he told us. "I never, never thought that that would happen. I really did expect to be here for three years." He had been reassigned to a Richmond high school by Superintendent Jewell-Sherman. It was, she said, a business decision. "There is a vacancy at a high school that Boushall feeds into. Parker's the best man for the job."

Boushall would have a new principal, its fourth in eight years. Madieth Malone was angry. "A lot of our kids are disappointed," she said. "Many of them have very inconsistent environments. The school is one place that they can come and be assured that things will be consistent. Instability, once again, is being created in a school where our kids are so fragile they don't need that instability."

144

The superintendent was unmoved. "He's not their father; he's their principal."

Land tried to rally the troops as he said goodbye. "I think we're right there on the doorstep, and I hope that when we get our scores back, you invite me back to celebrate, because it's going to be a nice celebration. It's going to be a really special, sweet celebration when we make those federal standards and those state standards."

All summer long, Land and Boushall waited for the results, but there would be no celebration. The scores dropped to a 55 percent pass rate in English and a 46 percent pass rate in math. No $8,000 bonus for Land. And no "turnaround" for Boushall, which remained on the warning list.

Superintendent Jewell-Sherman, soon to leave Richmond to teach at the Harvard Graduate School of Education, was matter-of-fact about Boushall's test scores. "We'll analyze it and move from there. That's part of public education in these United States."

Madieth Malone, soon to retire, was upset. She felt Boushall had begun to change for the better. "The bottom line, that's what everybody looks at," she said. "They don't see the small successes; that's what I look at. I have to look at kids who were not coming to school who are coming, kids who were not working who are working. Kids who are smiling more, who are enjoying school more."

Despite the scores, Land agreed. "I think the school year has improved. I'm not going to say I've seen a big change, a drastic change, 180-degree turnaround, you know, but I have seen improvement."

So had Parker Land failed as a turnaround specialist?

"I wouldn't feel personally that I've failed," he said. "I've learned an awful lot. I've learned that our kids, a significant number of those kids are in crisis. And there's a level of support that's needed that we just haven't realized yet."

Parker Land wasn't the only one of Virginia's turnaround specialists to struggle. Fourteen of the program's 21 principals at the time failed to meet federal standards for improvement. All made three-year commitments, but more than half either changed schools or left the program entirely after little more than one year.

Is the turnaround specialist approach flawed, superficial or inadequate? Maybe so. At least we can say that the concept has evolved. The newest wrinkle, borrowing the business concept of enterprise zones, calls for "partnership zones." The Massachusetts-based organization Mass Insight Education & Research Institute is leading the way. To quote from its literature, the partnership zone project is designed to "use the leverage and urgency of school turnaround to transform urban education and help thousands – ultimately millions – of disadvantaged children develop the skills they need to be successful in 21st century America. ... This is not incremental reform. The Partnership Zones will create and put in place new systems, new structures, and new approaches, but unlike most efforts to undertake real transformation in public education (e.g., the charter movement), it provides a plausible change–management pathway to bring it about *at scale* and (at least partially) *from within the system*."

While this sounds as if these new reformers may have learned lessons from the turnaround specialist approach, I again suggest we hold our applause.

12

Education's Four Gaps

It says here that public education's main problem is not the "achievement gap." What we have is more complex: It's an *opportunity gap*, an *expectations gap*, an *outcomes gap* and a *leadership gap*—not enough committed school boards and not enough strong school leaders.

Consider the gaps in order. Until we distribute resources more fairly *and* staff our schools with adults who expect the best from every child, we will continue to have big gaps in performance. When a principal works hard to dig up extra resources to close the opportunity gap, he or she is halfway there. But resources do not equate completely with opportunities; that is, they are necessary but not sufficient. We've all heard the stories (some of them true) about districts and schools in poor areas that are spending—usually by court order—an additional three, four or five thousand dollars per child without any discernible effect in achievement. 'Throwing money at the problem' is the disparaging phrase, but don't let that obscure the fact that money, resources, and opportunity matter.

Closing the *expectations* gap requires hiring teachers who expect the best from every child, and getting rid of those who don't believe in their students' possibilities. As former Mount Vernon superintendent Ron Ross notes, "When we talk about student achievement and an achievement gap, we generally focus on the students. That's wrong. You're never going to close it by that. Focus on the teachers."

Hiring carefully, mentoring young teachers, and firing when it's necessary eliminate any expectations gap. Then, magically, the outcomes gap is virtually certain to disappear.

Kids often have an intuitive understanding of the expectations gap. As one student in a successful school said, "I think in the other schools, it's the teachers' fault that the students don't do well, because the teachers sometimes expect good scores from the white kids, but from the black kids they just say, 'Nah, he's not going to learn as well as the white kids.'"

I once asked teachers in one successful school how they managed to get all kids over the bar. What they said struck me as a primer for successful teaching and learning. Their comments included:

"First of all, you don't give up. You try a number of strategies to develop a rapport with the child, which could be just sitting down after school and having a conversation."

"A lot of times being punitive with a child isn't going to be successful. You have to have rules, but punishment is not necessarily the thing you want to go to the first time, and perhaps even the second time, to get your point across."

"Always capitalize on the parts children do well. All children do something well, and if you praise them and capitalize on just that little bit, I think you can get some growth from them."

"Let them know that you really care about what they're doing correctly."

"If I am not getting through, the teacher that had the child last year is the one I go to and ask, 'What was successful with this child? What did you do that really worked?'"

"As a younger teacher, I'm always looking to the other teachers for advice, and everybody always has ideas to help me out."

"The most important thing is to not to make the child who's not getting it feel embarrassed. You have to do it privately. Go over it again at lunchtime. You do things with them by themselves. Treat them with the respect that you want back."

Right now states, school districts, politicians and educators focus almost entirely on the *achievement* gap. They create compensatory programs with all the best intentions in the world, but that exercise is doomed to failure. The gap won't disappear if one day poor and minority kids score at the same level as whites and well-to-do kids. And isn't it fundamentally racist to assume that white is the measuring stick against which to judge all others?

It's like judging Head Start by comparing Head Start kids to preschoolers of middle- and upper-middle-class families. The latter are going to keep moving up, because those families know about the importance of early stimulation. Then, because those who are well off keep moving up, it's easy to conclude that Head Start has failed. That's wrong. If, instead, we had some rational set of expectations for Head Start, we could judge its success or failure against that set of standards (are kids healthier, do they know the alphabet and the sounds of letters, and other questions).

White performance on standardized tests shouldn't be the standard against which others are judged. Instead, we need to do the hard work of setting standards, which requires even more hard work from us in advance. And we need to debate deep questions, including, "What does it mean to be educated?" and "What skills and knowledge does one need in order to be productive, lead a satisfying life and contribute to the greater good?"

The policy of "closing the achievement gap" between racial groups is doomed to failure, because school performance is closely linked to socio-economic status. As a group, children of the poor – whatever their color – don't do as well in school as children who grow up eating well; living in warm, clean homes;

and being cared for by parents who read to them, limit their television time and take them to museums.

The latter are born ahead and, individual success stories to the contrary notwithstanding, schools by themselves aren't going to close the gap. Nor will they ever catch up – after following a cohort of 4 million American children from birth to preschool enrollment at age 4, the National Center for Education Statistics notes that: "The percentage of children who were in a center-based setting increased as parents' highest level of education increased. For example, 43 percent of children about 4 years old whose parents' highest level of education was less than high school were enrolled in a center-based setting, compared with 71 percent of their peers whose parents' highest level of education was any graduate or professional school."

Stressing a racial achievement gap allows educators to rationalize their own performance, as in "I taught it, but they – *those* children – didn't learn it." A healthier approach involves setting clear, measurable standards and then providing whatever resources are needed to ensure that all measure up. For example, when I was at Dartmouth, we had to pass a physical education test, including swimming 100 yards, in order to graduate. We didn't have to swim it faster than someone else; we just had to swim it, and instruction was available for those who needed it. It was a realistic, clearly defined standard, for both students and coaches. And no coach could have said, "I taught them swimming; it's not *my* fault that they're at the bottom of the pool."

That we also have a *leadership* gap is demonstrated by the existence of one outstanding school in the middle of the poorest neighborhood, an island of excellence surrounded by schools that are mediocre or worse. It's a failure of leadership that the successful school is ignored or tolerated, instead of becoming the model for the rest of the district.

Too often educational leadership does not know that diffusing successful innovations is what they should be laser-focused on doing. Or, if they do know *what* to do, they don't know *how* to do it.

Why is it that most teachers don't have opportunities to visit each other's classrooms in their own building, let alone visit outstanding schools in their district that have been profiled in the local and national media? The leadership at every level in school districts does not encourage teachers and principals to take the time to learn from the best. It rarely rewards or recognizes those who are learning from others.

The leadership gap is defined not by words, but by inaction. It is leaders who do not have and do not implement strategies for identifying and learning from best practice, regardless of how much they talk about the importance of best practice.

School boards contribute to the leadership gap by not demanding more. Why are their expectations for their own results, including those of their superintendents, so low, when they are surrounded by examples of best practice in the schools and districts all around?

Ninety percent of the Fortune 1000 corporations wouldn't exist today if their leadership had thought and led as most of America's education leaders have over the past 30 years. The diffusion of innovation, and the daily effort to accelerate the pace of diffusion, is the lifeblood of these companies.

Hard work is part of the recipe. Our worst schools need outstanding leaders who will be on the job 24/7, until the schools can climb out of the hole. "And even when schools are performing, they require strong leadership," Ron Ross said. "Anyone who wants to excel shouldn't expect to go home at three o'clock. I tell anyone who gets into education, 'If you're coming in here because you think it's a 5- or 6-hour job with summers off, do me a favor. Find something else to do with your life.'"

151

In the beginning, local citizens ran their public schools, an arrangement that continued for more than 50 years. By the early years of the 20th century, though, more than 100,000 school districts had sprung up, and many of the amateurs in charge were hiring their friends as teachers, principals, custodians and every other job. In response, a class of professional educators emerged, and it ran schools for the next 70 or 80 years.

By the 1980s, dissatisfaction with education and the professionals in charge was palpable. Districts began reaching outside the guild to hire retired military generals, prosecuting attorneys, politicians and business leaders to run school districts. This achieved only occasional success, most notably in Seattle under retired Army Major General John Stanford.

In the 1990s, states took more interest in managing schooling. Some set standards and mandated exams for adults and children. Many passed laws allowing a new form of school management called "charter" schools: institutions that were allowed to manage themselves. But significant improvement continued to elude the system.

The search for a better way to run schools took a new turn when President George W. Bush proposed, and Congress passed, No Child Left Behind. That law meant that Washington told schools how to run things: more testing, new requirements for teachers and free tutoring. How poorly that turned out is evidenced by the fact that almost no one in Washington even refers to NCLB any longer; instead everyone except for hard-core Bush defenders calls it by its original name, the one that dates back to Lyndon Johnson. The Obama administration says it's all about ends and outcomes. It talks about "loose" controls of the process, but close or "tight" attention to the results. Now, with a divided Congress, it's probably all about gridlock and posturing. This is not the time to look to Washington for solutions.

With all due respect to educators and politicians, I think the situation calls for a new and radically different philosophy. I have a modest proposal for new leadership: Put the fire chief, the swimming coach, the band director or the highway engineer in charge of public education.

A competent fire chief manages resources responsibly. He can't put the best equipment and most of the firefighters in one neighborhood. In fact, rather than distributing firefighting resources equally, a competent chief puts them where and when they are needed. Put a fire chief in charge of education, and the best teachers would be in the neediest schools – at least until the "educational fires" were extinguished.

It seems to me that too many educators rationalize student failure by saying, "We taught them the material, but they didn't learn it." That's why I suggest putting a swimming coach in charge of schools. A swimming coach would never dream of patting herself on the back if even *one* of her students were found floating face down or lying at the bottom of the pool. With a swimming coach calling the shots, teachers would have to show results, which would force them to develop methods that worked.

When a high school has a dozen National Merit Semifinalists, nobody pays much attention to how everyone else is doing. That's why it makes sense to put a band director in charge. No capable band director would boast about the band's performance if only the trumpets played well but the percussion and woodwind sections were out of tune or off the beat. Band directors pay attention to everything: music selection, individual training of musicians and teamwork. They encourage individual talent but at the same time acknowledge that the whole *is* greater than the sum of the parts.

A competent highway engineer would also be a distinct improvement. After all, highway engineers design highways with one major goal: to get travelers to their destination. Thus, they make lanes about one-third wider than the cars, to allow for occasional inattention and wandering. They anticipate mistakes, and they design systems to prevent accidents. By contrast, schools play "gotcha" in classrooms, penalizing students for mistakes and, increasingly, telling them to go back and start the trip over. They are designed to sort students, not to see that all succeed.

If these proposals seem fanciful, I ask you to imagine educators, with their operating philosophies, working as fire chiefs, highway engineers, band directors or swimming coaches. Make a school administrator your fire chief, and the nicest neighborhoods would have all the fire engines. Put an educator in charge of highway design, and interstate highway lanes would be one inch wider than cars, perfectly designed to punish any and all driving errors. If the school superintendent is directing the band, cover your ears! As for letting someone who says "I taught it, but they didn't learn it" become a swimming instructor, let's not even go there.

Let's be honest about this. No fire chief, highway engineer, band leader or swimming coach would take the job, because running a school system is just about the toughest task imaginable. So we'll have to push for a change in attitudes by the people now in charge. They need to learn to think, and act, like the fire chief, etc. Then we'll have the public schools our democracy needs.

There's no silver bullet in education. The recipe for success includes some mix of strong leadership, committed teachers, an integrated curriculum, the willingness to challenge conventional wisdom and accepted practices, and the moral imperative to care for and about all of our children. *Real change requires real change.* You cannot snip off one loose end and expect genuine improvement; nor can you change one faulty policy and expect a new world. This is tough work.

13

Making Schools Safe

One spring day, our friend Kathleen stopped by on her way home from retrieving her 12-year-old son's backpack, which he'd accidentally left in his classroom at school. Her son Joey, a bright, thoughtful, somewhat quiet boy, is the target of relentless bullying by the jock majority on campus. Why are the jocks picking on him? Because he loves to read and is often seen carrying a book.

That's too bad, you might say, but isn't bullying a normal but unfortunate part of growing up? Isn't it something that kids work through, and maybe even manage to build some character in the process? Well, I've got a lot to say about that, but I'm not done with the story yet.

As I said, Kathleen went to her son's classroom to pick up his backpack. While she was there, she ran into the mother of one of Joey's classmates, who observed that Kathleen had only her younger child with her. "So where's Joey?" quipped the woman. "Home reading *War and Peace*, or something?"

We talk of 'the natural cruelty of children' as a kind of given: a rite of passage of sorts that's unfortunate but normal, and that we expect kids to either work through or grow out of in time. But what of this adult response – this tacit approval of, even participation in, the kind of "deliberate cruelty" that's been damaging and scarring millions of children in schools across our

155

country for years and years, and now seems to be getting worse with new technologies available and the advent of cyberbullying? This kind of heartless adult response is all too common. And when adults don't step in and actively work to stop bullying, they become a serious and sometimes deadly part of the problem. At the very least, their absence and willingness to ignore the situation creates a vacuum, in which a vulnerable child stands alone, and into which a bully (or a gang of them) easily steps and begins to fill the void with cruelty.

Schools spend hundreds of millions of dollars trying to ensure the physical safety of their students. They install metal detectors, hire security guards, pay for administrator and teacher training programs, and implement all kinds of other measures to create physically safe learning environments. This effort and commitment is laudable, and physical safety is important, but the real issue – the underlying one that paves the way for physical violence and for some victimized children to take their own lives to escape bullying – is *emotional* safety. That's what adults need to pay attention to. And that's where adults are really failing.

Did you know that between 60 and 90 percent of school children have been bullied, and at least 20 percent of students are bullies, according to some studies? Or that "chronic victims of bullying, bullied once a week or more, generally constitute between 8 and 20 percent of the student population," according to a 2009 U.S. Department of Justice publication for police officers?

Or that, in a major study called "Bullying and the Gifted," researchers reported that by eighth grade more than two-thirds of gifted students surveyed had been victimized? Or that in a recent study of California third- to sixth-graders, about 90 percent said they'd experienced bullying, and 59 percent admitted to bullying others?

Or that every day about 160,000 children miss school because they're afraid of being bullied, according to the National Association of School Psychologists?

And because most incidents of bullying go unnoticed by adults and unreported by the victims, the numbers I've just given you are probably pretty low compared to reality.

Ted Sizer, the late school reformer, once told me: "What you should worry about are the kids who seem to take pleasure in harassing and insulting other kids. The bullies, the ones who see school as a game and are constantly pushing the limits … Those kids need to be dealt with."

That's true. And besides all the obvious reasons we should worry about bullies (the children who suffer at their hands, the "bystander" children who observe abuse and are affected by it, etc.), there's a flip side regarding the bullies themselves. Sizer said what he most worried about were students who took pleasure in tormenting others – and their actions and influence move out from the schoolyard into the community at large.

According to "Bullying in Schools," a 2009 U.S. Department of Justice publication created to educate police officers about bullying:

> It is not only victims who are at risk for short- and long-term problems; bullies also are at increased risk for negative outcomes. One researcher found that those elementary students who were bullies attended school less frequently and were more likely to drop out than other students. Several studies suggest that bullying in early childhood may be a critical risk factor for the development of future problems with violence and delinquency. For example, Olweus' research found that in addition to threatening other children, bullies were several times more likely than their nonbullying peers to commit antisocial acts, including vandalism, fighting, theft, drunkenness and truancy, and to have an arrest by young adulthood. Another study of more than 500 children found that aggressive behavior at the age of 8 was a

157

powerful predictor of criminality and violent behavior at the age of 30.

According to "Bullying in Schools," bullies tend to grow up and have children who also become bullies. In other words, bullying engenders bullying, which engenders bullying, which engenders bullying. It's like that image of the snake with its tail in its mouth, forming a perfect circle; there's no end without first breaking the circle and then sending the snake on its way.

The fact is, most bullying between students is verbal, rather than physical. It's the so-called "normal" teasing that kids inflict on each other. So how does bullying begin? Usually it starts in an atmosphere lacking in emotional and intellectual safety.

As a reporter, I meet students all the time who talk openly about being teased:

"I'm just sick of some people making fun of me because of the color of my skin, or because of what I wear," said Jessica, a young white girl in a nearly all-black middle school in New York City.

"Kids would make fun of my ears, because they're big, and I just hated it," said Charles, 17 years old and about six feet two inches, recalling painful years of merciless teasing by classmates.

"They call me stupid, stuff like that, because I get nervous and start stuttering," said Carlos, a Maryland high school student, describing how other students reacted when he tried to read aloud.

"They'd go 'Hahaha, A.D.D. boy, you can't do anything right. You're so stupid,'" said John, who'd been diagnosed with A.D.D. and was on Ritalin.

Students tell their stories to me, a reporter from outside. I often ask, "What happens if you complain to teachers or to your parents?" Usually, the kids tell me, the adults say: "Get tough. That's just normal, so get used to it."

I've heard that before. I remember one of my daughters coming home after being cruelly teased at school. I was concerned enough to visit the head of the school. When I related my daughter's experience, he nodded. "We're aware of it," he said, "and we're watching to see how it turns out."

His detached attitude and his unwillingness to stop the bullying infuriated me. "Why isn't it your job to intervene?" I demanded.

"This is a natural part of growing up," he said, unfazed, "and kids have to get tough." We took our child out of that school, because we could. Why keep a child in an institution whose leader believes in going with the flow, instead of taking responsibility?

Add to that attitude the new "advances" in bullying, via social networking sites like Facebook and MySpace, cell phones, text messages, etc., and you've got an atmosphere that sparks the same old cruelty to spread like wildfire.

Deborah Meier, founder of the world-renowned Central Park East Secondary School, believes that most teachers and adults tend to dismiss teasing as normal, something children just have to adapt to. "We turn our backs," she said, "because we don't know what to do about it."

Meier believes that non-violent teasing and other cruelties are directly connected to physical violence. She insists that adults have a duty to become involved, and to intervene on behalf of those being harassed. "A truly safe school is willing to tackle the tough issues," she said. "Teachers are confident enough and powerful enough to say: 'Stop everything! We're not going to move until we have made sure this isn't going to happen again.'"

But what happens when adults aren't available, or able, or – since children tend not to report bullying – even aware of a bullying situation, and therefore don't help those being victimized? Various outcomes are possible, depending on the child and the situation, but tragically they can include the worst imaginable.

Phoebe Prince, 15, who transferred in fall 2009 from a small village in Ireland to South Hadley High School in Massachusetts (enrollment 700-plus), and was described as a smart, charming, popular girl who loved to read, was found dead by her 12-year-old sister in January 2010. She had hanged herself with her new Christmas scarf (a gift from the young sister who found her) after three months of relentless taunting and physical threats by schoolmates, both in person and through her cell phone, on Facebook and by text messages. Amazingly, the bullying continued after her death, with many cruel comments posted on Phoebe's Facebook memorial page. Nine teenagers, three of them juveniles, were indicted in spring 2010 in connection with Phoebe's death. No adults were charged, despite the inexplicable and disgraceful inaction of an unknown number of teachers and administrators at the high school who were – according to the district attorney – aware of the harsh bullying and yet did nothing.

Days after Phoebe's death, a 9-year-old boy named Montana Lance was found hanged in a school bathroom at Stewart's Creek Elementary School in Lewisville, Texas, an apparent suicide. The school district said that bullying was not involved. CBS News reported that friends from school said the boy was frequently teased. "He was just bullied too much," Keeley Blackwell, who walked home with the boy on occasion, told CBS station KTVT-TV. "Some of the things that people would say were harsh."

Two months later, Jon Carmichael, 13, hanged himself in his family's barn in Joshua, Texas. "Most of the school" bullied Jon, according to a classmate (who said that he'd also bullied Jon, but that they were both "just messing around"; the classmate added that he wished he could take back the things he'd done, but said he knew he couldn't).

Bullying impacts all kinds of children, from all walks of life. Some of the harshest bullying is directed at students who are gay, or even just perceived or rumored to be gay. These children's problems are often overlooked, and most teachers have not been prepared to cope with them. I asked Ramon Gonzalez, a brilliant young math teacher in a New York City middle school who was also studying to be a superintendent, about his awareness of students who might be gay. "Now I'm starting to be aware of the issue," he said. "It's hard for me to deal with because I grew up in a very traditional environment, so I'm trying to come to terms with that for myself. I've asked my counselor, 'What do I do?' And they don't know what to do either."

It's clear that bullying negatively impacts all children one way or another. Even those who are not direct participants in a bullying situation (neither the bully nor the victim, but instead witnesses and bystanders) are affected; studies indicate that only 10 to 20 percent of children who witness an act of bullying step in to "provide any real kind of help." Many of these students are probably afraid to get involved, but what kind of training for the future, and what feelings of intimidation, guilt or powerlessness, does that foster in kids who witness the abuse? Children and adolescents can be extremely cruel; bullies probe for soft spots and attack where they find vulnerability. Parents need to know how the adults in charge respond.

As I've said, a lot of trouble goes unnoticed – unless you know where to look and whom to ask. Talk to students. Ask them about the places in school where they feel unsafe, and check them out for yourself. Bathrooms are a good place to start, because if some kids are being bothered, there's a good chance you'll read about it there. Look for graffiti that singles out kids in a mean or threatening way.

Having lots of adults – and not just security guards – around can minimize violence and harassment, if the adults do their jobs. In safe schools, the teachers maintain a presence in the halls. They're around talking with students, not as policemen but as responsible adults. Unfortunately, some collective bargaining agreements place limits on the time teachers can be asked to spend in the halls. To my mind, this is a good example of what should not be negotiated – or what needs to be. In excellent schools, teachers know most students by name and want to be in contact with them because they genuinely like them, not just because they feel like they need to keep an eye on them.

Cyberbullying, the bullying that travels through technologies like social networking sites, cell phones, and text messages, ups the ante. Consider the following from the U.S. Justice Department's "Bullying at School:"

> The Internet creates opportunities for cyber-bullies, who can operate anonymously and harm a wide audience. For example, middle school, high school and college students from Los Angeles' San Fernando Valley area posted web site messages that were ... full of sexual innuendo aimed at individual students and focusing on topics such as 'the weirdest people at your school.'
>
> The online bulletin boards had been accessed more than 67,000 times [in a two-week period], prompting a sense of despair among scores of teenagers disparaged on the site, and frustration among parents and school administrators. ... One crying student, whose address and phone number were published on the site, was barraged with calls from people calling her a slut and a prostitute.
>
> A psychologist interviewed for the *Los Angeles Times* remarked on the harm of such Internet bullying: "It's not just a few of the kids at school; it's the whole world. ... Anybody could log on and see what they said about you. ... What's written remains, haunting, torturing these kids. The imbalance of power here was not in the bully's size or strength, but in the instrument the bully chose to use, bringing worldwide publication to vicious school gossip.

So how can adults – who don't move in the same cyber-circles or have the same skills or understanding of new technologies as today's children – better understand cyberbullying? The National Crime Prevention Center warns that this phenomenon is similar to classic forms of bullying in that it can lead to a loss of interest in school, a drop in grades and even depression. But cyberbullying is harder to run from and potentially more destructive, the site points out, because:

> It occurs in the child's home. Being bullied at home can take away the place children feel most safe.
>
> It can be harsher. Often kids say things online that they wouldn't say in person, mainly because they can't see the other person's reaction.
>
> It can be far reaching. Kids can send emails making fun of someone to their entire class or school with a few clicks, or post them on a website for the whole world to see.
>
> It can be anonymous. Cyberbullies often hide behind screen names and email addresses that don't identify who they are. Not knowing who is responsible for bullying messages can add to a victim's insecurity.
>
> It may seem inescapable. It may seem easy to get away from a cyberbully by just getting offline, but for some kids not going online takes away one of the major places they socialize.

Elizabeth Englander, director of the Massachusetts Aggression Reduction Centers at Bridgewater State College, gives some good advice in Emily Bazelon's article, "Could Anyone Have Saved Phoebe Prince?" "The best thing parents can do," Englander says, "is simply to start a conversation with their children." The article continues:

> Ask teens and tweens where they go and what they do online. Ask if they've seen hurtful postings or texts. Ask what they'd do if they did.

Schools can jump start this process by giving parents advice about how to respond, so they don't feel like they're fumbling around in a brave new world they don't understand.

If all of this sounds obvious, well, that's the upside. These efforts take awareness and effort and commitment on the part of schools and parents, but they're not technical or particularly difficult – you don't need to open [a] Twitter account to help your kid navigate the online world. That's a relief, because cyberbullying and traditional bullying are increasingly tangled up with each other.

Cyberbullying can be stopped. Adults have to set the right tone in a school. They have to intervene instead of standing on the sidelines. They have to empower children rather than simply shutting down computers, for example. Above all, they must pay attention. And in order to know what to watch for, parents must understand that in many ways the face of bullying is changing.

Schools are supposed to be safe havens, physically, intellectually and emotionally. We may not need anti-bullying laws (although about 40 states now have them) because of laws already in force that require school leaders to act. Bernice Sandler, one of the forces behind Title IX (1972) holds that view. Title IX prohibits sexual harassment, and most bullying falls into that category, she explains. "Most cyberbullying and other forms of bullying, as well, include sexual references. Girls are called 'sluts' and 'hos,' boys are called 'fags' and other sexual names. Sexual rumors and comments are frequent."

Dr. Sandler says Title IX *requires* schools to act, no matter where the cyberbullying occurs. "This federal law also prohibits these behaviors outside the school, as when personal computers are used, and when the behavior is disruptive to learning, such as affecting a student's ability to partake of the opportunities for learning in school as well as partaking in other school opportunities provided by the school. Schools have an obligation to stop sexual bullying when it occurs and to have a policy that prohibits it."

In other words, if an educator learns about it—no matter where it's happening – it's his or her responsibility to act. Nancy Willard, the attorney cited in the *New York Times* article about the Massachusetts case, argues that if off-campus behavior, including on-line behavior, "has or reasonably could cause a substantial disruption at school or interference with students rights to be secure," then educators have the authority they need.

She adds, "These cyberbullying incidents combine online and off-line altercations – and sometimes they turn violent or they result in school failure. Thus, reasonable adults could come to no other conclusion that school officials must be able to respond."

Jean Alberti says it's time for speaking the truth. Cyberbullying and other forms of bullying are nothing less than child abuse. "Change the label," she says. "The behaviors that constitute bullying--pushing, shoving, hitting, stealing possessions, taunting, teasing, ridiculing, spreading lies or rumors--if done by an adult would be labeled physical or emotional abuse. These would constitute a crime and would be prosecuted."

Why a double standard? she wants to know. "By not punishing bullying abuse, by not conveying that this is unacceptable behavior, children are learning that it is acceptable. As adults, they continue to bully others – at home and in the workplace – and the problem multiplies exponentially."

If bullying is really a form of abuse and if values matter, why not build schools around the concept of choice and variety? That would mean embracing the true mission of education, going beyond 8a.m.-3p.m., test scores, athletics and college admissions.

What if a district embraced differences and variety and choice, but at the same time insisted that each school develop its own code of conduct, of acceptable behaviors?

Publish the choices and the code of ethics/behavior, and let families make informed choices.

Me, I would put emotional safety at the top of the list of priorities.

What also should be publicized is the reach of Title IX. Dr. Sandler concludes optimistically. "I strongly believe that most educators want to stop cyberbullying, but many do not know what to do. Title IX has made a huge difference in sexual harassment and other forms of sex discrimination at many schools at all levels. It can make a difference in cyberbullying too, if educators knew about it."

Perhaps what's needed is adult training in how to intervene, as well as sanctions for failure to intervene. Just as adults are required by law to report suspected sexual abuse, so too should they be required to act in clear cases of bullying.

School leaders cannot split hairs and decline to get involved. It's their job, like it or not. How they respond matters, and the key is to be pro-active, not wait until something awful happens.

First consider how non-public schools function. Most have a code of conduct, one that their students must accept. So if a student from Andover, St. Joseph's or Pencey Prep does something on a weekend that is an egregious violation of the behavior code and is caught, that student would suffer the consequences. No way the school head could drop that "not my responsibility" line and get away with it.

And parents and students at these schools are made aware of the rules, which are spelled out in detail. As Patrick Bassett, the head of the National Association of Independent Schools, notes, "Parents and students are often required to sign a document indicating that they have read and agree to the expectations as specified in the Student Handbook."

Bassett says public schools can copy this approach. "Any school, public or private, can make character a core element of its standards and program. Any school that doesn't do that fails to educate the whole child. The 3 Rs of the academic curriculum must be accompanied by the 3 Rs of the character curriculum: respect, responsibility, relationships."

The more we understand about bullying, and the more accessible we are to help children who are being victimized, the safer we can make our schools and communities. Here are some concrete steps:

1. Allow children and youth to express their feelings.

Many will want to talk. Others may need to express their fears through drawing, working with clay or other nonverbal mediums. Try not to make value judgments, or tell them it will go away, or let them believe that a tragedy will never happen again. Their fears may not be realistic, but they are real. Acknowledge their concerns and let them know that grief hurts. Also, assure them that adults will take care of them.

2. At the same time, model tolerance and understanding.

America is an increasingly diverse country, and many schools enroll students who do not "look like us." Now more than ever, adults must protect those who are different. They must not turn a blind eye toward teasing and harassment of any sort, but particularly not the kind that involves a student's faith or ethnic background. Passions run high today, and ignorance must not be allowed to rule the classroom or the playground.

3. Listen and show children you care by providing extra attention and physical contact.

Touching and holding are comforting for very young children. If children experience great distress over a situation, now or later, seek support from appropriate counseling services.

4. Answer questions with simple, accurate information, and do not go into morbid detail.

Teachers may need to answer the same questions over and over as children seek reassurance. It is okay to say, "I don't know" and "I wonder about that, too." There are no magic "right" words, but there also should be no questions that are out of bounds.

The key point here is that schools embrace values, and that is a 24/7/365 proposition.

14

Charter Schools

When two roads diverge in a yellow wood, in poetry and in life, one must choose. After picking a path to follow, inevitably you ask the unanswerable question: What *would have happened* if you had chosen the other path?

Now we know what happens, at least in education, thanks to a remarkable study of charter schools in New York City. And that study, released in September 2009, suggests that it's time to widen *one* of the roads.

Because New York City doesn't have enough room in its charter schools, admission is by lottery. Over the past seven years, only about half of the 80,000 students who have applied have been accepted. Most of the others ended up going to traditional public schools in their neighborhoods.

Not only were the applicants similar in observable characteristics of race, gender, poverty, disability and English proficiency, but, because all had made the effort to enroll in a charter school, researchers could infer similarity in motivation and family interest in education. Such an opportunity is what the study's principal investigator, Caroline Hoxby of Stanford University, calls "the gold standard" in research: the opportunity to compare apples to apples.

The announced results were dramatic. The lottery winners went to 48 public charter schools, and those who finished eighth grade performed nearly as well as students in affluent suburban school districts in math, and about two-thirds as well in English. Every year in a charter school mattered, the study found, and by the end of eighth grade, what the researchers call the "Harlem-Scarsdale achievement gap" had been narrowed by 86 percent.

Overall, each year in a charter added about 5 points to math and English language arts scores on state exams, compared with those who lost the lottery. Every year in a charter increased a student's likelihood of earning a state Regents diploma by 7 percent.

The study's results can be generalized, Professor Hoxby maintains, because most charters are in cities, most urban districts use a lottery system and New York's students resemble urban students everywhere.

But, as with all education research, *caveat emptor* is a good rule to adhere to. For one thing, nowhere in the published study does Hoxby reveal how many children actually went through eight years in charter schools. She does, however, acknowledge that she did a fair amount of extrapolating.

Just what does that mean? Think of an 8-mile road race in which only *some* runners go the entire distance. Most, however, run only a portion of the distance — miles 1 through 3, say, or miles 5 through 7. And then the race officials compile the final standings by assuming that those partial race times would have been replicated over the full distance. If someone who ran only 3 or 4 miles of the course got a trophy, there'd be an uproar, of course, but statisticians like Hoxby are comfortable drawing inferences about academic performance.

But did she extrapolate beyond what the data support? Some in the field are skeptical of the study's conclusions. They note that the research hasn't yet been peer-reviewed, and that the study's scope, confined to New York City charters, limits its usefulness on a national scale. A few also point out that Hoxby's studies of charters tend to be consistently positive. But Hoxby stands behind her results and their meaning. What's particularly relevant to her, she says, is whether someone can articulate an actual problem with the methodology.

Meanwhile, her research shows that not all charter schools are the same. That is, there are clear performance differences among New York City's charter schools. While Hoxby will not name the best and worst, she is willing to identify the characteristics of the high-performing charters: a longer school day and year, more time devoted to studying English, pay based on performance and not simply on seniority and credentials, a clear academic mission, and a moderate disciplinary policy of both small rewards and small punishments (meaning that behavior issues, good and bad, are attended to on the spot). Every student of this movement immediately recognized that she was referring to KIPP schools.

Not all the charters were successful, though. Fourteen percent of students in the study attended charter schools that had an overall *negative* effect on math performance, compared with students who did not win the lottery.

So what does all this mean for choosing education's road to the future? What will happen now? Hoxby sees these results as a clear call to create more charter opportunities, something President Obama, Secretary of Education Duncan and many others have been urging. And not just words are involved. Race to the Top dollars went only to states that encouraged charter schools, and about 15 states modified their limits on charter schools in an effort to win that competition.

The general public clearly wants more charter schools – 64 percent in the 2009 PDK/Gallup poll on education are in favor of charters. And a 2009 survey conducted by *Education Next* reports that 52 percent of public school teachers support charters, a number that jumps to 60 percent when respondents are told of President Obama's support.

Parents want charter schools, too. In Washington, D.C., one-third of school-age children attend charter schools, the result of parents voting with their feet. In Los Angeles, only 10 percent attend charters, but enrollment jumped by one-fifth in 2009 alone. In other cities, parents are demanding more choices, more charters.

But, that support notwithstanding, charter schools are not home free. To understand why requires some history.

Although the notion of chartering schools had been around for a few years by 1988, it was in October of that year that the movement to legalize charter schools was born, at a small meeting by the headwaters of the Mississippi River in Itasca, Minnesota. Among those in attendance were two New York educators, Albert Shanker and Seymour Fliegel; Ember Reichgott Junge, a visionary Minnesota state senator at the time; and Minnesota educators Joe Nathan and Ted Kolderie. The concept of a charter – a renewable license to innovate, free of most school district rules – was built on a simple idea: Educators would be free to carry out their dreams, but would be held responsible for results.

I ran that meeting and remember well the overriding spirit of optimism. Chartering would be embraced by school districts, which would use them to "incubate" best practices. That has rarely happened, unfortunately. Most districts have resisted the idea of weakening their central control. And because charter teachers would no longer be obliged to belong to a union, Shanker came to see them as a threat to union power and declined to support the legislation that Senator Reichcott introduced in the legislature after the meeting.

Still, the idea had legs, in part because people could read into the term 'charter' what they wished. Some on the political right supported charter schools as a wedge to break up the public school monopoly, while others on the left thought charters would be the equivalent of their own private schools. Allowing profit-making firms to create charter schools, encouraged by state laws, produced more support.

The first charter school opened in Minnesota in 1992, with fewer than 100 students; today, 4,900 charter schools in 39 states and the District of Columbia enroll over 1.6 million students – and counting. Many of the charters have been granted by entities other than the local school district (the State University of New York grants charters in New York state, for example), effectively ending district monopolies.

Leading the way have been nontraditional educators like former New York City Schools Chancellor Joel I. Klein, Superintendent Paul Vallas of the Recovery School District in New Orleans, and former Chancellor Michelle Rhee in Washington. In the latter city, about 30 percent of students are in charters, and well over half of Vallas' schools are charters, enrolling more than 60 percent of his students. Throughout their tenure, these three leaders encouraged charters not as "incubators" but as challenges to the rest of their schools.

Still, as Nathan, a founder of the movement, says, "Some terrific charters are doing great things for kids, but charlatans have entered the field and have ripped off kids and taxpayers." He says charter school organizations must develop better ways of screening out crooks and incompetents *before* they get to start schools. He adds: "I see the charter movement, at its best, as an expansion of the civil rights movement, in which some of us participated. It's worth noting that Rosa Parks spent part of the last decade of her life trying to help create charters in Detroit. Some African-American and white families have asked for help in creating a charter in Topeka, Kansas, in the same school building that Linda Brown was not allowed to attend in 1954. ... Sadly, the local school board in Topeka turned down this request. The hostility of some professional educators towards charters today echoes the hostility we faced 30 years ago when we began trying to offer other options within public education."

Kolderie, another founder, believes unions are coming to terms with the idea. He cites a United Federation of Teachers initiative in New York City, teacher cooperative schools in Milwaukee, and the charter organization Green Dot Public Schools in Los Angeles as evidence that "when teachers play significant professional roles, the massive contracts generated by a boss-worker model are no longer required."

A trend that disturbs some is the propensity of wealthy individuals to adopt and support charter schools. To cite the best-known case, wealthy hedge fund managers like Julian Robertson Jr. and Whitney Tilson have made large contributions to charter schools in New York City. The Robin Hood Foundation, which raises many millions for worthy causes from Wall Street, lists charter schools as one of its top priorities. Are they supporting these schools to spur the system to improve, or to undermine it? UFT president Michael Mulgrew told the *New York Times* that their support was "all well and good," adding, "I would wish they would do it in a more foundational way, a way that would help all children instead of just a small group."

The ground keeps shifting under this movement, but two issues remain: quality control and persistent opposition.

For one thing, the Obama administration has embraced charter schools with great enthusiasm. Now, it's true that Secretary Duncan adds a qualification, saying that they support "good charter schools," but that strikes me as, for the moment anyway, an empty distinction, largely because of an absence of ways of measuring quality.

It's true that egregiously bad charters get shut down, but mediocre ones keep plugging along, doing just as much damage to kids as mediocre public schools. But what the charter school proponents don't seem to realize is that these mediocre institutions are also damaging "the movement." I've heard them (and you know who you are) say that mediocre public schools aren't punished, as if that justifies not closing mediocre charter schools. But it's no justification precisely *because* charter school advocates are claiming to be different. They cannot claim to be different and then act like the systems they are so critical of.

In fairness, several hundred charter schools have shut down over the past few years, which is the way it's supposed to work. And today we see regular public schools being closed because of persistent failure. That's something that never happened before charter schools existed!

Then there's the issue of opposition to charter schools. Everyone knows that unions have fought against charter schools because they've seen it in their self-interest (teachers in charter schools don't have to belong to unions). But guess what – local school boards have been as great a roadblock, and in some cases, even fiercer opponents. They go to court to keep charter schools from opening or expanding. Why? It's about money and control, as far as I can tell. As a December 2010 report from the Brookings Institution noted, "Charters generally operate on a tighter public budget for current expenditures than traditional district schools, receiving by one estimate only about 80 percent of the per pupil amount received by district schools, and by another only about 60 percent." But if the demand exists for charter schools, why shouldn't elected officials whose mandate is education be supportive?

Often they are not. For example, in fall 2009 in Los Altos, California, a county judge ruled against a charter school and for the local school board. The charter school had sued because it wanted to expand to include seventh grade and needed space to do so. Forget for a minute the particulars of that case and ask yourselves why it wanted a seventh grade. Could it be that parents

175

of sixth graders wanted to keep their children in the charter school? And why are school boards so hostile to success? Shouldn't they be trying to figure out what that successful school was doing, so they could copy it? That was the hope of charter schools, that they'd be incubators.

If you and I both operated restaurants, and mine was drawing a crowd and yours wasn't, wouldn't you want to know why? Wouldn't you think seriously about changing some aspect of what you were doing?

Or would you behave like many in the education establishment and sue me or try to shut me down? In other words, what can be done to change school board behavior? Is it all about money and power?

Just as the waters of Lake Itasca flow into the Mississippi and down to the Gulf of Mexico, expect the movement that began there to continue to grow. However, just as the Mississippi is a dangerous and sometimes unpredictable river, the charter movement should not expect smooth sailing.

Because the New York City study will – quite properly – produce more enthusiasm for charters, it's important to remember that 14-percent negative effect on math cited above. A buyer-beware attitude is more important than ever. Never forget that the word 'charter' on a schoolhouse door reveals no more about a school's quality than the word 'restaurant' on a sign tells you about the food inside. There's no substitute for transparency, high standards and direct observation of the sort reported in Hoxby's remarkable study.

Conclusion

My premise is simple: To solve public education's problem, we first must give it a name.

Deep down some of us just *know* that *great teachers* are the key. We know it because of a teacher in fourth grade who encouraged us to keep on drawing. Or a 7th grade social studies teacher who brought history to life and convinced us that politics could be honorable. Or the homeroom teacher in high school who always took time to listen but also insisted that you do your best. Because of a special teacher or two, when you hear about education's problems, you know deep down that all would be well if today's schools only had more great teachers like those.

On the other hand, suppose you are one of the millions who gave up on teaching, frustrated by its pettiness and daily humiliations. You might still be in front of a classroom if conditions had been different. And so you *know in your heart* that the root of education's problem is the job and its lousy working conditions.

That's the dilemma, and the ongoing battle: *Are mediocre teachers the heart of education's problems? Or is it the job itself, with its low pay and even lower prestige?* Those two very different analyses of education's problem are competing for domination, and whoever gets to define the problem is likely to control education policies for many years.

If the problem is mediocre teachers, the solution is obvious: if they cannot be retrained, replace them with better teachers. Today this *better people* approach seems to be gaining favor, spurred on by *Waiting for Superman*, Oprah, NBC's Education Nation and more.

Many in the *better people* group believe that smarter and more dedicated teachers are more likely to come from Teach for America than from traditional schools of education. The leaders this group have been Superintendent Paul Vallas in New Orleans and Joel Klein and Michelle Rhee, the recently departed Chancellors in New York City and Washington, D.C.

In New Orleans, more than half of the teachers under Paul Vallas' authority are members of Teach for America. Teach NOLA, a local version of TFA, has sent Vallas more than 400 teachers since 2007. It's a rare school in New Orleans that doesn't have at least one, and many have half a dozen or more teachers from TFA and TeachNOLA.

When she was Chancellor in Washington, D.C., Michelle Rhee eagerly recruited from TFA, not surprising since she got her start in education with TFA. When Rhee took the job in 2007, her mentor Klein gave her direct advice, "You have to get rid of people." And she did, firing or replacing several hundred teachers and over half of her principals.

Rhee's director of personnel told the *NewsHour* that at least 50% of the Washington teaching corps had neither the skill nor the motivation to succeed. On one level, that's an odd criticism, because isn't it the job of leadership – Rhee and her team, including her director of personnel – to provide motivation? Or is criticizing them for lack of motivation supposed to act as a motivator?

The competing *better job* view holds that the problem is with the job itself: teachers aren't respected, classes are too large, administrators don't punish unruly students, and so forth. Therefore, the solution is to make teaching prestigious, rewarding, and attractive – a job worth fighting for. "Give teachers a clear set of outcomes and expectations, the tools they needs, decent working conditions, and the time and trust that other professionals take for granted," the logic goes. That approach will

178

solve most of education's problems.

Some evidence supports this view. Because teaching doesn't offer much prestige, authority or pay, upwards of 40 percent leave teaching in five years.

While the argument about professionalism is compelling, it's mostly talk. Contracts negotiated by unions and school boards provide an operational definition of *better job*. It generally means higher pay, a shorter day, smaller classes, and a quicker path to tenure. Some contracts allow teachers to arrive a few minutes before school starts and leave a few minutes after the closing bell. Contracts may sharply limit the number of faculty meetings or require that the teachers give their permission before principal may enter the classroom. This narrow, trade union definition obviously favors teachers, but it's difficult to see how it benefits students—or elevates teaching to the status of profession.

In Washington, the *better people* argument seems to be winning. Race to the Top language rarely refers to making teaching a more desirable occupation. Secretary Arne Duncan, a supporter of Teach for America when he led Chicago's schools, has endorsed alternative teacher training pathways and criticized schools of education for low standards. He and the President support linking teacher pay and student performance, and the Department is encouraging testing in areas beyond Language Arts, Math and Science.

There's an inescapable irony here. Just as a *better job* has been narrowly defined by numbers (more money, fewer students), *better people* are also defined by numbers. Although adjectives like 'dedicated,' 'hard working' and 'uncomplaining' are thrown around freely in conversation, the bottom line is test scores. That's what *better people* do in the classroom—they move the needle.

And therein lies a flaw in the *better people* approach. Because even if they do move the needle, the vast majority of teachers from Teach for America are unlikely to stick around beyond their 2-year commitment.

Suppose for the sake of argument that 20 percent of our teachers are no longer willing or able to do the job. That's 400,000 teachers who ought to be removed and replaced, if efforts to retrain them fail. But if they are replaced by men and women who themselves depart after a few years, the system remains a revolving door, with one group of 'better' people replacing another.

A more sensible path entails redefining *better job*, but that won't be easy. Narrow and restrictive union contracts must be negotiated away or overturned, so that principals will not have to bargain with their teachers about coming into their classrooms, for example. The same school boards that agreed to idiotic and restrictive contracts favoring teachers now must have the courage to say no. Both boards and unions need to somehow put the interests of children first.

Teaching will be a *better job* when principals have authority over hiring their staff but are savvy about bringing trusted veteran teachers into the process.

It will be a *better job* when teacher evaluations of students count at least as much as the score on a one-time standardized test.

It will be a *better job* when employment contracts are not for life and employee evaluations are fair and thorough, with all due process rights respected.

Teaching will be a *better job* when everyone's pay depends in part on how students perform academically. However, merit bonuses must go to the school's entire staff, so that the art, music and physical education teachers and even the school secretary have a vested interest in success. There's no need to add standardized testing in more subjects. Instead, create conditions that encourage phys ed teachers, for example, to build math into their classes. (Don't just throw the football but graph the results for distance and accuracy.)

Teaching will be a *better job* when we recognize that the world has changed, and the job of a teacher is to help young people learn to ask good questions, not regurgitate answers. With the flood of information around them, young people need help separating wheat from chaff. And it's no longer the teacher's job to tell them the difference, but to give them the skills to inquire, to dig deeper.

When teaching becomes the *better job* as described above, the brain drain will no longer be a problem – and we will likely discover that many teachers *now* in the classroom have been *better people* themselves all along.

Chapter Notes

Introduction

Writing the introduction to this book was a trip down memory lane, back to the wonderful years I spent at National Public Radio. Because I had my own series, *Options in Education*, I was free to explore a wide range of topics that came under the umbrella of education (and that encompasses just about anything). And so I was able to spend many weeks in juvenile institutions. The NPR series that grew out of that experience, *Juvenile Crime, Juvenile Justice*, won the George Polk Award in 1982.

Later I became curious about how children with mental problems were received and treated. The ensuing 2-part series, *Children in Mental Institutions*, got my program thrown off the air in parts of Texas because of its harsh language, but it also caught the ear of Fred Rogers, who wrote me a complimentary letter about it. Fred and I became friends, and my children spent many hours in "Mr. Rogers' Neighborhood." He was a great American, and I miss him still.

As talk of a possible merger between the two big teacher unions heated up in the mid-to-late-70's, I just called the two union presidents up and asked them to 'debate' on my program. Both agreed. However, Albert Shanker of the American Federation of Teachers won these debates so convincingly that the National Education Association dropped out after three years.

Chapter 1 – The Influence of Teachers

It's odd and fascinating how student memories persist. I can call back strong memories of my time in Mr. Sullivan's English class, but I recall very little about math or Latin or history. Years later I wondered whether O Henry actually said, "Turn up the lights," and not "Turn down the lights," but Mr. Sullivan presented the quote as a paradox, which made it intriguing fun to wrestle with.

I have more specific memories of being a student than I do of my two years as a high school teacher. For example, many years later I was attacked in a blog by someone, apparently a former student, for not having served in Vietnam. (I was ineligible because of my spinal fusion and major knee surgery.) That blogger asserted that I had introduced the war poetry section by having some students carry me into my classroom in a closed coffin, whereupon I opened the top and sat up, waving an American flag. Now *that* I am pretty sure I would remember doing, if I had done it!

I went into teaching with literally no training whatsoever. I like to think that my energy, enthusiasm and willingness to burn the midnight oil made up for my ignorance of the art and skill of teaching, but of course, that could be wishful thinking on my part.

Chapter 2 – Learning to Read

The National Assessment of Educational Progress reports are a good source of information on reading. Look at the 2007 results as well as the most recent ones. Two other sources may be of interest as well:

C. Juel, "Learning to Read and Write: A Longitudinal Study of 54 Children from First through Fourth Grades." *Edu-*

cational Psychology 4 (2008): 437-447 and C. Juel, P.L. Griffith, and P.B. Gough, "Acquisition of Literacy: A Longitudinal Study of Children in First and Second Grade," *Journal of Educational Psychology* 78, no. 4 (1986).

My interest in reporting about reading probably stems from watching and helping my own three children learn. My year in the two classrooms is carefully documented in *Early Learning* on PBS (1996). When it aired nationally, the principal was shocked (although many wondered why she hadn't seen it happening during the year). She arranged for her teachers to take summer classes in reading instruction, and she put all the children from the young woman's class into Johnny Brinson's class for the next year – where they learned to read! See learningmatters.tv.

Incidentally, Fannie C. Williams Elementary School now has a beautiful, colorful playground for the kids because of the national nonprofit community-building organization KaBOOM! which, according to its website, "envisions a great place to play within walking distance of every child in America." Visit kaboom.org.

Chapter 3 – Learning to Teach

There are a number of useful references here, beginning with our own TFA series, *The Real World of Teach For America: The Series* on our website at learningmatters.tv.

But I also recommend Steven Farr and Teach For America, *Teaching as Leadership: The Highly Effective Teacher's Guide to Closing the Achievement Gap* (San Francisco: Jossey-Bass, 2010). Amanda Ripley's fine article in the January-February 2010 issue of *The Atlantic*, "What Makes a Great Teacher?" is one you wish would never end, even though it's largely uncritical of TFA. Another 'must read' about teachers and their training is Elizabeth Green's "Building a Better

184

Teacher" in the *New York Times Magazine*, March 7, 2010. Green shows how serious, thoughtful on-the-job training can help most teachers do a better job. It's a thoughtful answer to those whose solution is wholesale firing.

I didn't know this about nursing, but at their formal pinning ceremonies, nursing students typically recite the Nightingale Pledge. Different versions of the pledge exist, but this particular rendition has two lines that strike me as also applicable to education:

> I will do all in my power to maintain and elevate the standard of my profession ... and devote myself to the welfare of those committed to my care.

In the interest of full disclosure: I have a doctorate in Education and Social Policy from the Harvard Graduate School of Education and have been a Trustee of Teachers College, Columbia University since 2001.

Chapter 4 – Serious Fun?

Have children's lives become so structured and overscheduled that they may now need "recess coaches" to stimulate their imagination and help them relax? For that chilling view, see "Playtime Is Over," by David Elkind, the *New York Times*, March 27, 2010, A17.

Here's one way to increase the 'serious fun' quotient: Teach the First Amendment, which reads "Congress shall make no law respecting an establishment of religion, or prohibiting the free exercise thereof; or abridging the freedom of speech, or of the press; or the right of the people peaceably to assemble, and to petition the Government for a redress of grievances." This is, arguably, the most important sentence in any of our essential documents and in our lives.

185

For more on this, see Sam Chaltain's book, *American Schools: The Art of Creating a Democratic Learning Community* (Lanham: Rowman & Littlefield Education, 2009).

Chapter 5 – Evaluating Teachers

This chapter went through many rewrites, because the ground here seems to be shifting very rapidly. How quickly the increased public awareness will translate into widespread change is questionable, because we have about 14,000 school districts—and therefore about 14,000 teacher/administrator agreements. But don't miss Daniel Weisberg et al., *The Widget Effect: Our National Failure to Acknowledge and Act on Differences in Teacher Effectiveness* (Brooklyn: New Teacher Project, 2009).

Two other references of import here: Scholastic and the Bill & Melinda Gates Foundation, *Primary Sources: America's Teachers on America's Schools* (Scholastic Inc., 2010) is a fascinating poll and worth your time. While it's not a scientific study, 40,000 teachers did respond to the blind questionnaire, perhaps motivated by the offer of a gift certificate for completing the survey. The process also included 12 focus groups and follow-up questions.

Met Life doesn't get enough credit for its annual reports, including this one: Harris Interactive and MetLife, *The MetLife Survey of the American Teacher: Collaborating for Student Success,* (New York: MetLife, 2009). Teachers may not get to observe each other teaching, but they say they collaborate a lot.

Nearly all teachers engage in some type of collaborative activity with other educators at their school each week. On average, teachers spend 2.7 hours per week in structured collaboration with other teachers and school leaders. Elementary school and secondary school teachers spend a similar amount of time each week in collaboration with others at their school, but the ways that they collaborate are different. At the elementary school level, collabora-

186

tion among teachers is more common within grade level (87% of elementary school teachers vs. 57% of secondary school teachers). At the secondary school level, collaboration among teachers is more common across grade levels, but within subject area (74% of secondary school teachers vs. 59% of elementary school teachers).

I admit to being intrigued by the Toledo Plan, even though it falls short when it comes to working with ineffective tenured veterans. But the bottom line question remains: If Toledo is weeding out 6-10 percent of first year teachers who aren't likely to be successful, shouldn't that produce significantly better teaching—and learning? The results in Toledo are generally better, but not dramatically so. Toledo is one of 8 large cities in Ohio, and its students do better than those in the other seven in most grades and most subjects, but Toledo's students still lag behind the rest of the state. On the most recent tests, for example, 64 percent of Toledo's 3rd graders were proficient in math versus 59.9 percent in the other 7 large cities and 76.9 percent statewide. In 8th grade reading and math, however, Toledo students scored below their peer cities, 39.0 in math versus 47.9 percent, and 34.3 versus 38.1 percent. The statewide averages were 64.2 and 68.8 percent.

PAR's continued existence is not guaranteed. In school year 2010-11 PAR was budgeted to spend roughly $300,000, an amount that's lower than in previous years simply because Toledo has been laying off teachers, not hiring new ones. But with Toledo schools facing a budget deficit of nearly $40 million (a levy failed to pass in November 2010), PAR could conceivably be on the chopping block. On the other hand, it has a track record for weeding out ineffective rookies and bringing newcomers into the profession in a way that infinitely superior to the old 'sink or swim' method. See our December 8, 2010 *NewsHour* report, "Evaluating Teachers: Are Teacher Unions the Solution?" at learningmatters.tv.

Using student performance as one piece of teacher evaluation is inevitable. New York, by the way, rewrote its (stupid) law in 2010, in order to qualify for Race to the Top funds, which it received. And Randi Weingarten, now president of the national union (the American Federation of Teachers), said in a December 2009 speech that her union was prepared to accept the use of test scores to evaluate teachers, provided adequate safeguards were in place.

As I say, the ground keeps shifting. In early December 2010 the Michigan State Senate passed a teacher evaluation bill, under which at least 45 percent of public school teachers' evaluations would be based on academic achievement growth of the students in their classrooms, as measured by standardized state tests and local evaluations. According to the *Detroit News* article, "Senate Reworks Rules on Teacher Evaluation," December 2, 2010:

> The bill, which passed 21-14, is designed to weed out bad teachers. It requires evaluations to label teachers as 'highly effective,' 'effective' or 'ineffective.' The remaining portion of evaluations would be based on school boards developing a definition of professional effectiveness. The bill now moves to the House for consideration. 'We will continue to lobby in the House" to defeat the bill, said Doug Pratt, communications director of the Michigan Education Association. 'This bill does nothing to decrease the time or cost of removing ineffective teachers from schools.'

The Obama Administration deserves credit for standing up to its traditional allies and not caving to pressure. When the Administration's Race to the Top threw down the gauntlet to unions and challenged them to participate in a competition for billions of dollars only if they agreed to develop plans to base teacher evaluation in part on student performance, most state and local unions went along. Now we will see whether they abide by what they have agreed to.

The *Los Angeles Times* continues to release data connecting specific teachers with student performance, and the heated reactions continue. My blog was overwhelmed with comments, two of which are below. The others are still posted at *Taking Note*. ("Proof that Teachers Matter," *Taking Note*, August 18, 2010, takingnote.learningmatters.tv.)

One thoughtful respondent made this point:

> The issue to me is much less about whether results should be public than whether or not teachers get the support they need to be effective. I came to teaching from business, and the biggest difference between industry and education is the degree to which people are set up for success. Sure there are some teachers, as there are folks in any profession, who won't be successful no matter what support they get. But in my experience of coaching teachers the past ten years, most teachers are significantly and measurably more effective when they receive high quality job-embedded coaching and training. Hold teachers accountable? Sure, as long as we hold schools accountable for providing them the support they need and deserve to be successful—just as management did when I worked in business.

To which I say, Amen.

My defense of the press elicited many attacks, including this one:

> The press (you) are not talking about the causes of what amounts to a symptom—failing schools are a symptom of an underlying disease called poverty. You can advocate all the school-side reform you can think of, and it won't do a thing because the factors that cause student failure don't exist at school, they exist at home. You want extraordinary teachers, but you must realize that at 34K to start, you get what you pay for. America wants schools to raise their kids for next to nothing. That won't work. And shaming and blaming won't work either. Actual concern for these kids, and policies that could actually help them are non-existent. Think universal health care, free early childhood education, better jobs, better housing, better services, music, art, field trips, spontaneity, recess, and teachers who care about children, not test scores. The media have a responsibility to discuss the truth. You failed.

To me this critique is a classic example of the best being the enemy of the good. Those poverty-stricken parents who don't have adequate health care are sending you their best kids, and they are expecting you to teach them. They're not keeping the best ones at home. Teachers make a difference in children's lives. To be blunt, I think people who throw up their hands and say they can't do anything (or anything much) because of the attendant social issues and problems that exist outside the school ought to find other work.

I mentioned Dennis Van Roekel's views on evaluation. Here's a short excerpt from my March 2010 interview (Listen to the podcast "How to Judge a Teacher," released April 2, 2010 on learningmatters.tv.):

> VAN ROEKEL: For example, in a class, you never know which part of a geometry lesson a class isn't going to get. If based on my assessments, a quiz or whatever, they didn't get my unit on slope, then what (administrators) should be watching for is what did I do as a result once I realized that they didn't know it? Did I adjust my teaching? Did I find a new way of doing it? That's what I should be judged on.
> ME: And if you didn't?
> VAN ROEKEL: If I didn't, I think that's part of the evaluation system.
> ME: So it's the practice, not the test score?
> VAN ROEKEL: Yes
> ME: But the test scores are the measure of the practice.
> VAN ROEKEL: *I don't believe that.*

Finally, what about the possibility that *students* are the best evaluators of teachers? In late December 2010 the preliminary results of a $45 million study of 3,000 teachers and their students in seven districts (including New York City, Memphis, Dallas, Denver and Pittsburgh) indicate a strong correlation between student achievement and student ratings. Students filled out confidential questionnaires developed by Ronald Ferguson, the

Harvard researcher involved in the study. He told the *New York Times*, "Kids know effective teaching when they see it."

Is this transferable? If students knew their ratings influenced how teachers were paid, would that change the teacher-student dynamic?

Chapter 6 – Paying Teachers

The battle is just being joined and will heat up when (and if!) the reauthorization of ESEA moves ahead. The Education Equality Project is pushing hard for connecting student performance and teacher evaluation. See its strongly worded "Open Letter to the President, Secretary of Education, and Congress on ESEA Reauthorization," published March 3, 2010, edequality.com.

How do teachers feel? According to "Primary Sources," the Scholastic/Gates Foundation survey of teachers referenced earlier, 36 percent of teachers say that paying for performance is not at all important and 25 percent say it is "absolutely essential or very important in retaining good teachers."

But don't forget that many teacher unions across the country declined to support their state's application to the federal Race to the Top program, reportedly because of that program's insistence on tying salaries to student performance. In Florida, for example, only 14 percent of unions signed a memorandum of agreement supporting the application.

And the backing away has already begun. For more, see "One System Backs Out of Race to the Top; Another Comes In," *Atlanta Journal Constitution*, November 17, 2010, and "School Districts Evaluate Merits of Merit Pay," a November 2010 report by the Hechinger Institute. If unions reject this one principle and some school districts say that Race to the Top programs will cost more than they're getting, then innovation will slow to its usual glacial pace.

Most of what Richard Rothstein writes is worth your time. This particular observation is from Elaine McArdle's "Right on the Money," *Ed.Magazine: The Magazine of the Harvard Graduate School of Education*, Winter 2010, 18. "How to Judge a Teacher," the April 2, 2010 podcast, can be heard on learningmatters.tv.

Chapter 7 – Keeping Teachers

For a comprehensive and mostly optimistic view of the future, see Barnett Berry and the Center for Teaching Quality, *The Teachers of 2030: Creating a Student-Centered Profession for the 21st Century* (Center for Teaching Quality, October 2009.)

In the *American Educational Research Journal* (September 2010) Richard Ingersoll asserts that the so-called shortage of math and science teachers is illusory. In an article asking "Is The Supply of Math and Science Teachers Sufficient?' he answers yes. "The problem is retention, not recruitment," says Ingersoll. "In the same year that Bush called for recruiting 30,000 STEM teachers, we had 26,000 quit. That's a terrible waste of talent." That conclusion, he admits, "is heresy" to most science educators and advocates."

It also has important policy implications. "When I started this work I assumed, like everybody else, that we have a critical shortage," he says. "And it was only slowly that I came to these contrarian views. Now I'm getting hate mail from people saying that I'm undermining their arguments to politicians and college presidents about the need to train more STEM teachers." (As reported in *Science*, November 2010).

And if you are really wonky on this issue, take a look at Richard Ingersoll and David Perda, *How High Is Teacher Turnover and Is It a Problem?* (Philadelphia: Consortium for Policy Research in Education, University of Pennsylvania, 2010). In a 2003 report, *Is There Really a Teacher Shortage?,* Ingersoll wrote:

The data also show that the revolving door varies greatly among different kinds of teachers and different kinds of schools. As found in previous research (Murnane et al. 1991; Huling-Austin 1990; Hafner & Owings 1991), the SASS data show that teaching is an occupation that loses many of its newly trained members very early in their careers—long before the retirement years. I used these data to provide a rough estimate of the cumulative attrition of beginning teachers from the occupation in their first several years of teaching. The data suggest that after just five years, between 40 and 50% of all beginning teachers have left teaching altogether. Of course, not all of this attrition results in a permanent loss of teachers. One form of this revolving door is represented by temporary attrition—teachers who leave teaching but return in later years, as discussed earlier (also see Murnane et al. 1991). But again, from the viewpoint of those managing at the school-level, temporary and permanent attrition have the same effect—in either case it results in an immediate decrease in staff, which usually must be replaced.

For more about the costs, see The National Commission on Teaching and America's Future, "Policy Brief: The High Cost of Teacher Turnover," June 2007.

Teacher education is a swamp, for the most part. An estimated 1,300 to 1,400 institutions prepare teachers; 632 belong to the National Council for Accreditation of Teacher Education, the membership organization that accredits teacher education programs. Another 100 institutions have applied for membership. NCATE distributes a list of "red flags," including degrees that can be earned in less time than at a traditional college, addresses that are box numbers or suites, and names that are similar to well-known, reputable universities. For more on NCATE, see ncate.org.

I also recommend Arthur Levine's report, "Educating School Teachers," (Washington, D.C.: The Education Schools Project, 2006).

Chapter 8 – Who Needs Tenure? Why Senority?

It's odd and frankly disturbing how much easier it is to get tenure in K-12 than in higher education.

I drew on a number of sources regarding tenure in K-12 schools, including the National Council on Teacher Quality, *2009 State Teacher Policy Yearbook: National Summary* (Washington, D.C.: National Council on Teacher Quality, 2009) There's an interesting chart, "Figure 70: How Long Before a Teacher Earns Tenure?" Also of value are Ingersoll and Perda, *How High Is Teacher Turnover and Is It a Problem?* (Philadelphia: Consortium for Policy Research in Education, University of Pennsylvania, 2010), and the Consortium on Chicago School Research at the University of Chicago Urban Education Institute, "More Than Half of CPS Teachers Leave Their Schools Within Five Years; African-American Schools Hit Hardest," news release, June 29, 2009.

In December 2010, the Wyoming legislature took up legislation that would eliminate teacher tenure. That same month, New York City moved to make it more difficult for teachers to attain tenure. It replaced the old system (a principal checked a couple of boxes!) with rules requiring that principals factor in a teacher's contributions in and out of class and his students' achievement scores. Under the old system, only 3.7 percent of teachers were denied tenure last school year. It was worse four years earlier, when just .04 percent were turned away.

Expect more attacks on tenure going forward.

Higher education is different. Tenured university professors can be fired, of course, but their due process rights, guaranteed under the Constitution, are stronger because of tenure. In 2005 the *Wall Street Journal* reported that between 50 and 75 tenured professors, out of 280,000, were dismissed for cause. That's about .03%, 3 one-hundredths of one percent!

194

But is the firing rate much higher in K-12? In Toledo, where the Toledo Plan gives teachers the power to evaluate each other, since 2004 only 15 tenured teachers have been fired, out of a teaching force of 2,000. That's not even three a year, about two tenths of one percent.

I know it's heresy, but I believe that institutions of higher education, especially graduate schools of education, need an alternative pathway besides the tenure track, 1-year appointments and adjunct and part-time teachers. Why not give out a significant number of *5-year* contracts to talented men and women who want to do cutting edge work at the intersection of teaching and policy and don't care about tenure and the accompanying restrictions of 'publish or perish'? This would reduce the institution's dependence on tenure, which has budget implications, and also attract a new breed of teacher.

Chapter 9 – Leadership's Revolving Door

Bill Roberti turns up twice in our *NewsHour* coverage; in St. Louis, "Turning Around St. Louis Schools," August 17, 2004, and in New Orleans, "Schools Before and After Katrina," November 1, 2005. Regarding New Orleans, Bill Roberti wrote to me in an email on February 19, 2010:

> We had two contracts. The first contract was with Orleans Parish School Board and was for total management and oversight; it had a Memorandum of Understanding with the state and I reported to an oversight committee. That was originally $16.7 million and was revised and extended several times. The second contract was post-storm with the state to open schools and oversee all the claims and insurance management as well as oversight of construction. That was for $29.1 million.

Clearly, Paul Vallas would rather that money had not gone to Roberti's firm.

Incidentally, the Broad Foundation provided the funds to pay for the Council of the Great City Schools analysis of St. Louis.

A general shout out here to *Education Week,* a vital publication. For leadership coverage, see *Education Week,* June 23, 2004, January 12, 2005 and March 9, 2005.

Chapter 10 – Following Leaders

Over my career I have spent a lot of time following leaders. For three school years, 1992-1995, we videotaped Diana Porter's efforts to persuade the faculty and staff at Woodward High School in Cincinnati to adopt Ted Sizer's Coalition of Essential Schools principles. The documentary, *The Fifty Million Dollar Gamble* (Learning Matters, 1996) is a compelling story of two-steps-forward, two-steps-back school reform, in which the status quo eventually triumphs.

And between 1994 and 2000, I followed David Hornbeck's efforts in Philadelphia, where he tried to implement a 10-part plan he called "Children Achieving." He ran into the buzz saw known as the Philadelphia Federation of Teachers, a union renowned for its rigidity and resistance to change. The resulting documentary, *Toughest Job in America* (Learning Matters, 2000), is still used in college courses for its object lessons in social change, teacher unionism and more.

And in school year 2000-01, we followed five rookie teachers in Brooklyn for what became a 7-part series that the *NewsHour* called *Making the Grade.* I think that may be the most popular extended coverage ever on the *NewsHour,* as viewers got invested in the trials and tribulations of Jack, Renee and the others. Jim Lehrer jokingly referred to it as "the PBS version of *Survivor.*"

My colleagues on the D.C. and NOLA stories worked at least as hard as I did, and probably harder. Cat McGrath and

196

Jane Renaud worked on the Washington story from day one. Valerie Visconti worked with at least three other producers on the New Orleans story. David Wald has assisted throughout, and we produced 12 episodes from each city.

We would not have been able to produce both had not those three foundations stepped up to the plate. A shout-out to Richard Laine and Lucas Held at Wallace, Marie Groark at Gates, and Karen Denne at Broad!

Not enough is known about Rhee's teaching in Baltimore. She told the *Washington Post*, "It was a zoo every day..." but she vowed not "to let 8-year-olds run me out of town." According to the *Post*, "She discovered learning improved when everyone sat in a big U-pattern with her in the middle and she made quick marks on the blackboard for good and bad behavior without ever stopping the lesson. She spent an entire summer making lesson plans and teaching materials, with the help of indulgent aunts visiting from Korea. She found unconventional but effective ways to teach reading and math. She set written goals for each child and enlisted parents in her plans. Students became calm and engaged. Test scores soared."

No one has been able to document those gains, leading her opponents to accuse her of deception. Apparently no records were kept; but her colleagues from those days recall her determination and hard work. See Jay Mathews' "Baptism by Fire Vulcanized Rhee, 'Brat Pack' Peers," the *Washington Post*, October 27, 2008.

Although Rhee has always given Mayor Adrian Fenty credit, the rest of the world wasn't as understanding. At the Democratic Convention in Denver in 2008, a *Newsweek* editor told me they were thinking of putting Rhee on the cover and asked what I thought. Bad idea, I said, because to be accurate you have to put Mayor Fenty on the cover with her. Without him, she's toast, I said, and she knows it. "We won't do that," the editor said. "It won't sell magazines."

Later, of course, *TIME* put the chancellor on its cover, all by herself. (See *TIME*, December 8, 2008.)

She got her *Newsweek* cover in December 2010 with the announcement of 'Students First,' the organization she founded. For a critical analysis of her new venture, read "Is Michelle Rhee Putting Students First?" Sam Chaltain, December 10, 2010, huffingtonpost.com.

Some D.C. teachers told us that Rhee blamed *TIME* for using that particular photo. One said, "What she said was that she actually took several pictures. They didn't display the pictures of her sitting around with several kids or her sitting in a classroom. Of course they're going to pick the actual picture that's going to get all the teachers all stirred up." But Rhee could have declined to pose with the broom in the first place.

But the broom was an accurate image, because by the end of the school year, she'd removed 36 principals, 22 assistant principals, and 121 employees in her central office. This is one reason that Randi Weingarten, president of the American Federation of Teachers, refers to Rhee and New York Schools Chancellor Joel Klein as the leaders of the "Blame Teachers First" movement.

(Klein left office on January 1, 2011, and went to work for Rupert Murdoch, developing educational innovations. His eight years produced significant structural changes and some improvement in graduation rates and academic performance. Another noteworthy legacy: at least five of his former deputies moved on to lead elsewhere, including Andres Alonso in Baltimore, Marcia Lyles in Delaware, and Chris Cerf in New Jersey.)

Even though Rhee was losing students, she professed not to be concerned. As long as kids were in a good school, she said on numerous occasions, she didn't care if it was one of hers.

Initially, the money for the higher salaries was to come from foundations. Down the road, Rhee said, she would find the money by cutting costs elsewhere. But before long, the

198

economy collapsed, jeopardizing everything. In the end, Rhee negotiated a contract that greatly reduces the power of seniority and gave teachers a large raise, retroactive to the date the previous contract had expired—three years earlier.

The NEA, the other (larger) teachers union, doesn't accept the idea that pay should be tied to student performance. Early in March 2010, I interviewed the president of the National Education Association. I began by asking Dennis Van Roekel, who taught high school math for 25 years, if a teacher could be judged in part based on how his or her students perform. He said no. (Listen to the podcast "How to Judge a Teacher," released April 2, 2010 on learningmatters.tv.)

Rhee and Fenty weren't the only political losers. George Parker lost his own re-election bid in November 2010, defeated by the union's vice president. Very few union members bothered to vote, so it's impossible to say if this was a repudiation of Parker, but his opponent, Nathan Saunders, often accused Parker of being 'too close' to Michelle Rhee.

A good source for more about Paul Vallas is "What Makes Vallas Run?" Grant Pick, *Catalyst Magazine*, December 1996. When he signed his contract, he told state superintendent Paul Pastorek that he would be going home to Chicago after two years. He probably told Pastorek that he'd go by train because he hates to fly. He often drove to Chicago to see his family, meaning that he'd spend most of his long weekend in the car.

Vallas, a member of the Greek Orthodox Church, is right at home among people of faith. Part of what drives him, he said, is his conviction that one must use his talents for good. To do otherwise is a sin, he believes.

Chapter 11 – The School Turnaround Specialist

Wouldn't it be great if someone compiled a history of education's pursuit of panaceas? The list would include subject matter specialization in math and science, the open classroom, busing, parental choice, learning styles and differentiated learning, computer-assisted teaching and learning, competency-based education, assessment-driven improvement strategies, charter initiatives, small schools and turnaround specialists. When will we ever learn?

The turn-around approach has its detractors, including Ted Kolderie of Education Evolving. He writes:

> Once again our national government is setting out to get America better schools and better learning. Once again, however, its effort starts inside the traditional 'givens' of school and learning. So again it will probably disappoint. The need today is for policymaking instead to open to *non*-traditional concepts of school and learning – and to find a theory of action that can accommodate this radical change.

For more, see educationevolving.org.

Here's more about the UVA program, in case you are interested. "The School Turnaround Specialist Program entails a close working relationship between district personnel charged with supporting school turnaround efforts – referred to as the district shepherd – and the principals who have been identified to participate in School Turnaround Specialist Program and initiate the school turnaround." Also, "In the spring of 2004, the Virginia Department of Education contracted with the Darden/Curry Partnership for Leaders in Education to design and implement the Virginia School Turnaround Specialist Program." The first program was small-scale, nine days in the summer, another few days during the year and some consultant visits. Today it's a two-year program. See darden.virginia.edu.

The UVA program adopted another business concept: financial incentives. Each principal in the first cadre got a $5,000 bonus upon completion of the training and development of their plans and – if test scores hit the turnaround targets – bonuses of $8,000 the first year and up to $15,000 the next two years. The state also agreed to provide participating principals $50 per pupil for critical items that contributed to the turnaround process.

Parker Land left the high school in 2008, reportedly "for health reasons." We have lost touch with him, I am sorry to say. I think he got a raw deal, if you really want to know.

Chapter 12 – The Leadership Gap

In my experience, effective schools with strong leaders do not shy away from practicing or teaching values. As Ron Ross notes: "Good schools teach character. We teach values. We have to teach the next generation how to get along with each other. If we don't do that, then we ought to close the schools, because I don't care how good you are on a test, if you can't live with your neighbor, then I don't think you've been taught."

"Is that risky business?" I asked him.

"There is a line that one doesn't cross," he replied. "I'm not telling students, 'You must be a Baptist' or 'You must be a Roman Catholic.' But we are saying, 'You must not fight, you must not cheat, you must not steal.' The schools are supposed to transmit the values of society, not just give multiple-choice tests. We wonder why so many kids are cheating, it's because they came from schools where they concentrated on a test."

Chapter 13 – Making Schools Safe

Incidentally, the top reason for being bullied is physical appearance, not gender or sexuality. However, according to

GLSEN, nearly nine out of 10 lesbian, gay, bisexual or transgender youth (86.2 percent) reported verbal harassment at
school due to their sexual orientation, 44.1 percent reported
physical harassment and 22.1 percent reported being physically
assaulted.

Are bullies insecure, deep down? Probably not. Bullies
do not appear to have much empathy for their victims. Young
bullies tend to remain bullies, without appropriate intervention.
Adolescent bullies tend to become adult bullies, and then tend
to have children who are bullies. In one study in which researchers followed bullies as they grew up, they found that
youth who were bullies at 14 tended to have children who were
bullies at 32, suggesting an intergenerational link. They also
found that '[b]ullies have some similarities with other types of
offenders. Bullies tend to be drawn disproportionately from
lower socioeconomic-status families with poor child-rearing
techniques, tend to be impulsive, and tend to be unsuccessful in
school.' In Australia, research shows that bullies have low empathy levels, are generally uncooperative, and, based on self-
reports, come from dysfunctional families low on love. Their
parents tend to frequently criticize them and strictly control
them. Dutch (and other) researchers have found a correlation
between harsh physical punishments such as beatings, strict disciplinarian parents and bullying. In U.S. studies, researchers
have found higher bullying rates among boys whose parents use
physical punishment or violence against them.

I am going to depart from form here and list a number
of valuable sources, for those readers who wish to dig deeper
into this complex issue. They are generally presented here in
the order their information is presented in the chapter.

Jean Sunde Peterson and Karen Ray, "Bullying and the Gifted:
Victims, Perpetrators, Prevalence, and Effects," *Gifted Child Quarterly* 50, no.
2 (2006).

Also see "Study: Gifted Students Become Bully Magnets," *Consumer Affairs,* April 4, 2006.

Rana Sampson, "Bullying in Schools," *Problem-Oriented Guides for Police, Problem-Specific Guide Series, No. 12,* (Washington, D.C.: Center for Problem-Oriented Policing, Office of Community-Oriented Policing Services, U.S. Department of Justice, 2009), 4.

Jean Sunde Peterson and Karen Ray, "Bullying and the Gifted: Victims, Perpetrators, Prevalence, and Effects," Abstract, *Gifted Child Quarterly* 50, no. 2 (2006).

Thomas Tarshis and Lynne Huffman, "Psychometric Properties of the Peer Interactions in Primary School (PIPS) Questionnaire," *Journal of Developmental & Behavioral Pediatrics* 28, no. 2 (2007).

U.S. Department of Education, "Lead & Manage My School: Exploring the Nature and Prevention of Bullying," ED.gov.

Susan Limber and Maury Nation, "Bullying Among Children and Youth," *Juvenile Justice Bulletin* (Office of Juvenile Justice and Delinquency Prevention, April 1998), Also, page 9 of the U.S. Department of Justice's "Bullying in Schools" discusses the vicious cycle and intergenerational aspects of this issue.

Jean Decety et al., "Atypical Empathic Responses in Adolescents with Aggressive Conduct Disorder: A Functional MRI Investigation," *Biological Psychology* 80, no. 2 (2009): 203-211.

John Roach, "Bullies' Brains Light Up with Pleasure as People Squirm," *National Geographic News,* November 7, 2008.

Susan Donaldson James, "Immigrant Teen Taunted by Cyberbullies Hangs Herself," ABC News, January 26, 2010.

Melissa Newton, "Police: Texas 9-year-old Boy Hanged Self at School," CBS News, January 22, 2010.

Transcript of Interview with Leticia and Chris Montelongo, "Bullying a National Problem?" *Anderson Cooper 360 Degrees,* CNN, interview aired April 1, 2010.

Rana Sampson, "Bullying in Schools," *Problem-Oriented Guides for Police, Problem-Specific Guide Series, No. 12,* (Washington, D.C.: Center for Problem-Oriented Policing, Office of Community-Oriented Policing Services, U.S. Department of Justice, 2009), 14.

Rana Sampson, "Bullying in Schools," *Problem-Oriented Guides for Police, Problem-Specific Guide Series, No. 12,* (Washington, D.C.: Center for Problem-Oriented Policing, Office of Community-Oriented Policing Services, U.S. Department of Justice, 2009), 11.

The National Crime Prevention Council, "What Is Cyberbullying?" Circle of Respect, http://www.ncpc.org

Emily Bazelon, "Could Anyone Have Saved Phoebe Prince? She Was Tormented by Bullies at School and Online. Here's What We Can Learn from Her Suicide." *Slate*, February 8, 2010.

Chapter 14 – Charter Schools

A competing study known as CREDO was released not long after Hoxby's research. It too came from the Stanford campus, but its findings were dramatically different. It says that only 17% of charter schools outperform comparable public schools, while 37% under perform their public counterparts. Critics of that study say that, after the first year, those disparities disappear. And Hoxby's report has been criticized elsewhere. See analysis by Stanford Professor Sean Reardon in his review of "How New York City's Charter Schools Affect Achievement" (Boulder and Tempe: Education and the Public Interest Center & Education Policy Research Unit, 2009.)

As noted in the chapter, a major goal of the founders was cooperation, districts working with charters to improve the system. Unfortunately, that almost never happens. But it may be changing. In mid-December the Minneapolis Star Tribune reported on what may be a trend, cooperation brought about by outside funding:

> The U.S. Department of Education awarded a $3 million grant over five years to a collaborative effort that includes the St. Paul public schools, several charters and the local business community. As part of the effort, organizations including Target, Travelers, the Minnesota Business Partnership, the University of Minnesota and the Center for School Change (CSC) at Macalester College in St. Paul will help with teacher and administrator training. In Minneapolis, public schools recently were awarded a $100,000 planning grant from the Bill and Melinda Gates Foundation for charter/district cooperation. The initial project will involve sponsoring training programs that are open to teachers from both systems. Minneapolis was among nine cities chosen for the planning funds that were deemed ready to get past the friction and operate in a more collaborative environment.

Sure, these sound a lot like fancy bribes to do the right thing, but so what!

Just how public are charter schools really? In a response to "The Road Not Traveled: Tracking Charter Schools Movement,"my December 1, 2009 post at *Taking Note,* the thoughtful reformer Deborah Meier sounds a cautionary note about the public purpose of public schools:

> The question is who is accountable for the whole – every last child. That's the purpose of public schools. Alas, the way charters have evolved it no longer seems to me that they accept that commitment, that definition of publicness. They more and more resemble the 'system' they were organized to disrupt – but without the same responsibility. We are not talking about innovative mom & pop stores, but large national companies, licensed by the state to operate with public money and very little public oversight or responsibility.
>
> Charters could have become more like the 'pilots' in Boston had we moved carefully together without using them for other purposes – such as busting a large public union, lowering the wages of teachers, ending 'governmental' monopolies, dividing the public into competing 'publics' etc. The immediate constituents of the school make fewer and fewer on-site decisions, and are less and less accountable to each other than under the mindless system that I assumed charters were intended to change.
>
> What next? Fire departments? Police? We've already begun to privatize prisons – maybe we'll call them charter prisons?
>
> Schools can be the centers of a revived public life – or another symptom of a disintegrating common purpose.

The question of whether charter schools are truly accountable is perplexing. We know that some get shut down, probably a lot more often than traditional public schools, but is that enough? Julie Woestehoff, the author of *Public Accountability and Renaissance 2010* (Parents United for Responsible Education, November 2008), says people aren't paying enough attention. She wrote in an email:

Fifty-seven schools or charter networks were sent Freedom of Information Act requests for board minutes, membership lists, and by-laws. Even after follow-up letters from the Illinois Attorney General's Office, more than two-thirds failed to respond to our FOIA requests. We concluded that these schools have no governing bodies, which violates the law and Chicago Public Schools policy. Within the smaller set of 18 responding schools/networks, we found, among other things, that only 7 of the 152 board members of the responding charter schools are parents, or less than 5%. The by-laws of most of the schools were in violation of the Open Meetings Act. Our research certainly does not support the claim that charter schools are 'more accountable' to the public.

She does not explain why she believes boards are the key. After all, parents who are dissatisfied can vote with their feet, an option that's usually not available in regular public schools.

Nelson Smith of the National Alliance for Public Charter Schools weighed in on accountability as well:

On the quality issue, there's been a considerable shift toward 'tough love' among the leadership of the charter movement in the past few years, and it's just beginning to show up in numbers. NACSA (the authorizers' group) points to a dramatic drop in the percentage of new approvals between 2003 and 2008 – it's getting a lot tougher to get a charter in the first place – as well as a striking increase in closures (either revocation or non-renewal) as well as a shift toward non-renewals for purely academic reasons. In Ohio this year, about 16 charters will shut down as a direct result of legislation that Ohio and national charter leaders asked for in 2006 (and yes, it takes time to compile the record on which to take action). The National Alliance for Public Charter Schools has committed to increase overall quality both by encouraging replication of high-performing models and by working with states and authorizers to get more aggressive in closing low-performers.

But you can't just wave a magic wand. One of the reasons the National Alliance created a new model state charter law is that in many states, the rules for intervention are opaque – and some authorizers don't take action because they fear they'll get sued. So states have got to hold these authorizers harmless if they do their job right.

I'm no fan of 'mediocre' charters either – but we need to distinguish between malingerers and schools that are struggling through startup, or that are pinched for classroom resources because they're paying 20 percent of income for facilities in a state that provides nothing. The preponderance of charters are in the mid-range of performance, and they need equitable funding and technical support to keep on an upward trajectory. It's a serious mistake to think that only a small group of charters are succeeding.
(*Taking Note*, "The Road Not Traveled: Tracking Charter Schools Movement," December 1, 2009)

There's some evidence that a few public systems are copying charter innovations. For more on this, see Mary Ann Zehr's story in *Education Week*, November 10, 2010, "Public Schools Taking Lessons from Charters." That would be wonderful.

For evidence of school board hostility, see "End of the Line," our *NewsHour* report about San Diego, aired August 15, 2007, where the school board battled long and hard – and ultimately unsuccessfully to keep two schools from becoming charter schools. Superintendent Alan Bersin lost his job because he defied his board.

My restaurant analogy (*Taking Note*, "The Road Not Traveled: Tracking Charter Schools Movement," December 1, 2009) drew a heated response from Monty Neill of FairTest:

The example of a restaurant is terrible. Schools are (still, most of them) public spaces, part of our (endangered) social commons. Restaurants are private. Public schools serve the common good through common ownership and decision-making. That is one of its great contributions to society and to democracy, the other being the education of citizens. Both are often not done well. Both, but particularly the latter, become arguments for charters. However, the evidence is that charters are on average worse, based on test scores.

But the first issue pertains to democracy and the role of common spaces such as schools in maintaining a democracy, and in part to how to exercise that well in face of often problematic school boards, low voter participation, etc. But that discussion is rarely raised, drowned out by proposals to eliminate or greatly curtail the power of school boards, or to the effective replacement by corporations (charters).

It seems that as schools are increasingly defined in only instrumentalist and economic terms (I just read a truly awful 'vision statement' for MA's schools). The idea of schooling for democracy heads toward disappearance. The marketization of control over education is the parallel phenomenon leading to the elimination of schooling as democracy.

A final note – I agree there are excellent and truly innovative charters. A few pose no harm to democracy and could spur innovation, something that has not been built into the system.

About the Author

John Merrow began his career in journalism as an education reporter with National Public Radio in 1974, where he created the weekly series, *Options in Education*, for which he received the George Polk Award in 1982. He is currently president of Learning Matters. Since 1985, he has worked in public television as education correspondent for the *PBS NewsHour* and as host of his own documentaries. His work has been recognized with Peabody Awards in 2000 and 2005, Emmy nominations in 1984, 2005 and 2007, four CINE Golden Eagles and other reporting awards. A frequent contributor to *USA Today*, *The New York Times*, *The Washington Post*, *The Los Angeles Times* and *Education Week*, he is the author of *Choosing Excellence* (2001), *Below C Level* (2010) and co-editor of *Declining by Degrees* (2005). He blogs regularly at *Taking Note: Thoughts on Education.*

Merrow earned an A.B. from Dartmouth College, an M.A. in American Studies from Indiana University and a doctorate in education and social policy from the Harvard Graduate School of Education. In addition to two honorary degrees, he received the James L. Fisher Award for Distinguished Service to Education from the Council for the Advancement and Support of Education in 2000 and the HGSE Alumni Council Award for Outstanding Contributions to Education in 2006. He was for many years a visiting scholar at the Carnegie Foundation for the Advancement of Teaching and currently serves as a trustee of Teachers College, Columbia University.

Made in the USA
Lexington, KY
08 July 2011